FLAT GREEN BOWLS

The Skills of the Game

FLAT GREEN BOWLS
The Skills of the Game

GWYN JOHN

THE CROWOOD PRESS

First Published in 1991 by
The Crowood Press Ltd
Gipsy Lane
Swindon
Wiltshire SN2 6DQ

British Library Cataloguing in Publication Data

John, Gwyn
    Flat green bowls: the skills of the game.
    1. Ball games: Flat green bowls – Manuals
    I. Title
    796.315

    ISBN 1–85223–511–X

Acknowledgements

My thanks to Richard Bray (British Isles Singles Champion);
Hatherleigh Bowling Club and members Derek Bryant, Derek
Gard and Jeff Horne; the Umpire, Max Richards; to Bodmin
Indoor Bowling Club, and Jimmy Davidson and Bowls International
for allowing the inclusion of the exercise 'Freezing the Head'. My
special thanks to my wife, Mayville.

Picture Credits

Bob Armstrong: Figs, 94, 95 and 97; Stephen Line: 2 and 98; Peter
Bradshaw: Fig 100; Department of Trade and Industry: Fig 101;
Fig 99: The Chronicle and Echo (Northampton).
Demonstration photographs by Tim Macaire
Line illustrations by Margaret Cree

Note   Throughout this book, the pronouns 'he', 'him' and 'his' are
intended to apply to both men and women. It is important in sport,
as elsewhere, that men and women should have equal status and
opportunities.

Typeset by Acorn Bookwork, Salisbury, Wiltshire
Printed and bound in Great Britain by BPCC Hazell Books,
Aylesbury

Contents

Gwyn John was appointed South West Regional Coach for the English Bowls Coaching Scheme in 1979 and National Director of Coaching in 1987. He has devised courses for training both instructors of beginners and coaches, which are now used at national levels. He has acquired his excellent coaching skills from his thirty-eight years in education – fifteen as a head teacher – and his extensive practical experience in bowling. In 1980, he reached the final of the All England Fours. For the past three years, he has been a regular contributor to the *World Bowls* magazine, presenting a series of articles covering all aspects of the game.

Harry Death, the Chairman of the English Bowls Coaching Scheme, and I were responsible for appointing the first members of the National Coaching Team of the English Bowls Coaching Scheme in 1979. Gwyn was an original member of that eight-man team, as the National Coach for the South West Region. He was so successful in that position that he was a natural choice to succeed me as Director of Coaching on my retirement in 1987 from the post. He has been kind enough to describe me as the 'Midwife' of the EBCS; if that is so, then I would comment that the growing child could not have been passed to safer hands than Gwyn's.

We still work together on the green at coaching clinics, youth schools and in the preparation of International Teams. On clinics, he has earned over many years the nickname 'Doctor John' for the patient way he cures all kinds of bowling ills. On youth schools, this former headmaster, earns the respect of his pupils for his deep knowledge of his subject. In International Team preparation, he brings to his work the fervour of his Welsh blood, although, like me, his earliest sports coaching was with a round football!

All bowlers and bowls coaches, from club level to international level will find a great deal to read, mark and learn from this book by a man I am proud to call a good friend and top-grade bowls Coach – indeed, I know none better.

Jimmy Davidson
Honorary Secretary, World Indoor Bowls Council

It has been a pleasure and a privilege to have known and worked closely with Gwyn over the past ten years, first in his capacity as Regional Coach to the South West and more recently as the National Director of Coaching and Development. His pleasing personality and command of communication makes him more than acceptable to all classes of bowlers from the beginner to the International. The English Bowls Coaching Scheme has, and continues to flourish under his leadership, and I look forward with anticipation to anything he may choose to write.

H.A.C. Death
Chairman, English Bowls Coaching Scheme

Introduction

A HISTORY OF THE GAME

A great deal has already been written about the history of the game of bowls. So popular was the game in this country that it incurred the wrath of monarchs to the extent that legislation was passed to ban the game. One of its most severe critics was

Fig 1 Clifford Craig.

Henry VIII. However, we have ample evidence that the game was in full flow during the reign of his daughter, Elizabeth I, and played by no less a person than Sir Francis Drake.

Drake's game on Plymouth Hoe is part of the history of the Armada. As a schoolboy once wrote, 'Drake delayed his attack because he was having trouble with his bowels'. It is hoped that this book will, in some way, help people have less trouble with their playing of the game.

Let us come forward some four centuries from 1588 and Drake's game, to arrive at the present day. Millions of people can now sit comfortably at home and watch televised bowls events. The impact of television has been remarkable and there are now thousands who wish to take up bowling; indeed it is now recognized as one of the fastest-growing games in the country. This huge influx of would-be bowlers includes an ever-increasing number of young people of both sexes, which once and for all explodes the myth that the game of bowls is 'Old man's marbles'.

The game of flat green bowls is now played throughout the year, both outdoors and indoors, and current membership figures are as follows:
English Bowling Association (EBA) 128,000
English Women's Bowling Association (EWBA) 45,929
English Indoor Bowling Association (EIBA) 90,000
English Women's Indoor Bowling Association (EWIBA) 38,000

Introduction

Fig 2   The determination of David Cutler.

Added to these, there are a number of bowlers now enjoying the short mat game which is convenient for sports halls and village halls as they only need to accommodate a mat that is 45ft (13.7m) long. This often creates an appetite for playing the game on a larger playing surface. Consequently, more and more people are participating in the game of bowls at all levels, on greens of various lengths and surfaces.

1 Equipment

THE BOWLING GREEN

Outdoor Greens

From May to September the game of bowls is usually played on grass surfaces (there are some outdoor greens that have a syn-thetic surface). Great care and specialist skill are needed to maintain these greens in order to provide a first-class playing sur-face that is as level as possible. The greens are square, with sides measuring from 40–44yd (36.6m). This playing surface is then divided into six rectangles or rinks as they

Fig 3   The rink.

are called. Each rink is usually 18–19ft (5.5–5.8m) wide although there may be regional variations. The right- and left-hand boundaries of the rink will be marked by strings drawn tightly between two white pegs set on the banks beyond the ditches and the pegs set at the four corners of the rink. The centre of the rink is shown by a numbered marker (each rink has to be numbered consecutively). This marker is equidistant from the right- and left-hand pegs set in the bank. Each end of the rink will be bounded by a section of the ditch.

The whole green is surrounded by a ditch, which can be from 2–8in (5–20cm) deep, and from 8–15in (20–38cm) wide. Rising from the back end of the ditch, there should be a bank in as upright a position as possible and not less than 9in (22.9cm) above the surface of the green. Such banks should not have steps cut into them, nor contain material likely to damage a bowl or jack.

Indoor Greens

From October to April, bowlers can play on an indoor green. Some of these are large enough to contain eight rinks while others can offer only two rinks, or even only a single rink. The playing surface can be of a variety of man-made fibres or of jute or felt.

Rinks can vary in width since indoor regulations allow them to be 12–13ft (30.5–33cm) wide. Indoor greens will not have the right- and left-hand boundaries marked with a string but will retain the markers at each corner of the rink and the numbered marker, which indicates the centre line and is the centre point between the right- and left-hand boundary markers. The requirements for the ditch and banks are very similar to those for the outdoor game. Information on this subject can be found in a 'Laws of the Game' booklet, which can be purchased by applying to the respective Secretaries for the indoor or outdoor game.

The popularity of bowling has increased so rapidly that some indoor clubs have had to limit membership, so a newcomer could find his or her name on a waiting list. In spite of the fact that the indoor game can be played in greater comfort and without bad weather conditions to hinder the bowler, there are still many who prefer the outdoor game with 'the sun on their backs'. Wherever you play, the important thing is that you enjoy the game.

THE BOWLS

Most bowls are now made of processed powdered plastic, and there is a bewildering array of different makes and sizes of bowls from which any beginner can select. Do not rush into an early or unwise purchase, as the financial outlay can be considerable. It is commonly believed that you should try to bowl with as large a size as is comfortable for a smooth and easy delivery action, with no strain, but do not err on the side of choosing a set that is too large, as you may find them difficult to control.

The size and weight of bowls must conform to the laws of the game and will range from size 0 ($4\frac{5}{8}$in/11.7cm) to size 7 ($5\frac{1}{8}$in/13cm), the weight increasing in proportion to the size. However, nowadays manufacturers are offering a heavyweight bowl, so the prospective purchaser can be faced with making a choice between, for example, size 4 normal weight or size 4 heavyweight. There are arguments for and against using a heavier bowl. The heavier bowl is less likely to be moved out of the head following contact by another bowl but it does require a

Fig 4   There are so many sets to choose from.

tighter control by the bowler when he delivers it. Some bowls have dimples or grips in a circular pattern around both sides of the bowl. Some players claim to be better able to grip the bowl because of these dimples. If you feel the same way, then by all means purchase such a set. Although all bowls that are manufactured have to conform to the Master Bowl, it is well known that some bowls will take a straighter line along the green, whereas others will need a wider arc of travel.

Most beginners will receive a barrage of well-intentioned advice. It could be that your coach might be able to help you with your selection. Also you will have had some experience of bowling with a borrowed set during the early coaching sessions and may wish to stick with a similar set. Do not choose a set simply on the basis that they look good or feel good in the shop. The only place to try them correctly is on the green, and you should do this before parting with your money.

Fig 5   A complete set of waterproof clothing.

Remember that just as with a racket, a golf-club or a bat, a set of bowls becomes an extension of you and, therefore, it is very important that you have confidence in them. Some bowlers will change their set after one season. Perhaps it has nothing to do with the bowls but simply that the bowler feels he may obtain better results with a different set. However, if you make your decision carefully, the bowls you select could be your 'good companions' for many years. Of course, there are some bowlers who may need to change their set of bowls for other reasons. Possibly they develop arthritis in the wrist or fingers, which dictates that a smaller set is necessary.

Having ascertained the differences between sets, then personal preference comes into operation. Whatever size, weight, make or colour you choose, remember that you must master them. Regardless of indoor or outdoor, rain or shine, the bowl in your hand will only perform as well as your skill will allow; therefore, be honest with yourself when you make your initial choice.

Fig 6   A duster or small towel for drying the bowl in wet weather conditions.

CLOTHING

Footwear

This must conform to the laws of the game. Remember that a game of bowls can take from three to four hours to complete. Therefore, it is essential that your choice of footwear be for comfort rather than anything else.

Dress

As a general rule it should be white above the waist, with grey trousers. Club matches or representative games may sometimes require you to wear white trousers rather than grey.

Waterproofs

It would be sensible, in view of the British summers, to acquire a good-quality set of waterproofs. Being penny-pinching in this area could result in some discomfort following or during rain, which in turn would affect your game. During wet weather some bowlers have a small towel, others a chamois leather, to dry their bowls prior to playing a shot. There are some bowlers who use neither of these and prefer to play the bowl wet. This is plainly a question of personal choice.

2 Taking Up the Game

It would be advisable for any newcomer to be introduced to the game by a qualified Instructor of Beginners, certificated by the English Bowls Coaching Scheme (EBCS). Many bowling clubs – both indoor and outdoor – now have a qualified instructor or coach. He or she will have available a selection of different-sized bowls to offer the beginner and will ensure you have any other equipment necessary for your first game. It should be mentioned at this early stage that, from the time you are accepted into a bowling club, you must agree to abide by the club rules, which are designed for the benefit of all. Your coaching sessions will probably follow a similar pattern to the following.

SESSION 1

The Delivery of the Jack

Your coach invites you to stand on the mat, which is always 24 × 14in (61 × 35.6cm), and pick up the jack. You bowl the jack towards the coach, who will be standing directly in front of the mat at a distance of

Fig 7   Careful laying of the mat.

Fig 8   The manner in which the jack is held is a matter of personal choice.

Fig 9   Holding the jack.

Fig 10   Holding the jack.

some 15yd (13.7m). Often in the first few minutes a new bowler will demonstrate a natural delivery action from the initial stance on the mat to the moment the jack leaves his hand. (It is important to note that the English Bowls Coaching Scheme considers it to be important that the natural delivery action is encouraged rather than any stereotyped version imposed.) It is a fact that most delivery actions are as individual as a fingerprint. This, of course, makes coaching more demanding.

From this first rolling of the jack, the coach will have some idea of your suppleness, balance and general control. Remember that the bowls coach could be faced with a group of people with ages ranging from sixteen to sixty-six, and so he must adapt the coaching to each individual, having borne in mind the physical capabilities of the pupil.

The coach then moves to your right and requests that the jack be delivered towards him. When you have done this to his satisfaction, he will move to your left and allow you to deliver the jack along a line towards him. This exercise helps you to become aware of the fact that, in order to bowl a good line, it is better to turn the whole body to face that line directly.

The Delivery of the Bowl

When the coach is satisfied that you have no real difficulty in delivering the jack, he will allow you to choose from a selection of bowls and find the one with which you are most comfortable. As you have not yet been given instruction as to the grip to adopt, you will be holding the bowl in the manner that feels natural to you.

There are two main grips: the claw and the cradle. However, between the two, there are a number of variations that can be

Fig 11   *A front view of the claw grip.*

Fig 12   *A side view of the claw grip.*

Fig 13   *A side view of the claw grip.*

Fig 14   *The cradle grip.*

Fig 15   The wrist needs to be strong for this type of cradle grip.

Fig 16   As in Fig 14, most of the hand is in contact with the bowl.

Fig 17   The stance of Richard Bray, British Isles Singles Champion.

Fig 18   A semi-crouch stance.

Fig 19   An upright stance with both feet on the mat.

adopted. A great deal will depend on the size of the hand or even the strength of the hand and fingers but, as a general rule, it is advisable for the player to have as much of the hand as possible in actual contact with the bowl so that it can be held upright and not leaning to one side or the other.

Before you are asked to deliver the bowl, the coach may request that you extend the arm and hand in which the bowl is being held and turn the wrist so that the bowl is pointing downward. The grip should ensure that the bowl will not fall out of the hand. You will then take up your stance on the mat.

Bias

After a demonstration of how to lay the mat correctly as in Law 24, the coach may ask you to imagine a line drawn up the centre of the rink (see Fig 21). The smaller disc on the side of the bowl must always be facing this imaginary line, regardless of whether forehand or backhand is to be used.

It may be of help if the coach stands to your right with feet astride and asks you to deliver the bowl between his feet. You will be allowed to deliver several bowls along this line before the coach moves to your left and repeats the exercise. Watch what happens to the bowl and observe the built-in bias making the bowl curve from right to left on the forehand for a right-handed player, or from left to right when bowled from the backhand of the same player (see Glossary).

During the early stage, it can happen that the delivery of the bowl is not as smooth as that of the jack. The coach must act immediately to correct matters, be it stance,

Fig 20 *An upright stance with the leading foot off the mat.*

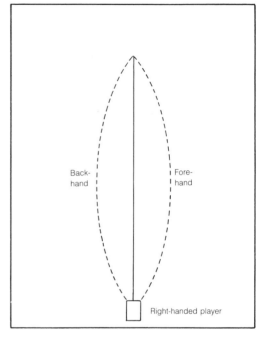

Fig 21 *The small disc on the bowl should always be facing the imagined centre line.*

grip, or the forward stride on delivery. When the coach is satisfied that you have developed a delivery action that is error-free, you can move on to the next stage.

Line and Length

The two most important factors in the game of bowls are line and length. Any bowler who wishes to execute a shot successfully must find the correct line and deliver the bowl with exact weight. The coach may set up the following practice: the jack is centred at three-quarter length with two

bowls at jack-high (*see* Glossary) but close enough to the jack that any bowl cannot run through (*see* Fig 23). You have to deliver two bowls on the backhand so as to reach the target. It can happen that the bowl makes contact with the target even though it was delivered with more weight than was necessary. The coach may ask you why the bowl was delivered with such pace or weight. He should allow the beginner to offer his own observations and/or reasons, then his thinking can be guided towards the speed of the arm coming through. It may be suggested that you practise this action without a bowl, as if you were going to bowl with sufficient pace to reach the far end of the rink, and then that you gradually slow down the action.

You can carry on this exercise with a bowl held in the hand but not released to

Fig 22 Too long a forward stride, causing the bowl to bounce.

give you an opportunity actually to 'feel' the amount of impetus you are imparting to the bowl. In order that you can practise both line and length, the two bowls will be moved away from the jack, leaving sufficient space for your bowl to pass through. Thus you are now made to concentrate on both line and length. All players like to achieve so early practices should be demanding but not too difficult, so that you are eager to return for the next session.

SESSION 2

This session begins with a reminder on correct placing of the mat. Then you go through a recapitulation of the exercises practised in the first session, i.e. rolling the jack to different lengths on the rink, followed by the jack being centred at three-quarter length with two bowls set at jack-high, presenting a wide target to the bow-

Fig 23 Finding the correct line using forehand and backhand.

ler. Your delivery action will be watched carefully because some little faults could have crept in. The coach aims to get the beginner's delivery action to be as smooth as possible.

The Shots

The coach can now place bowls in the head (*see* Glossary) so that he can talk about the different kinds of shots in the game.

1. draw
2. trail
3. yard on
4. positional
5. ditch weight
6. rest
7. wrest
8. blocking
9. wick
10. plant
11. split
12. promotion
13. opening up
14. drive or firing

These shots are described in full in Chapter 4. Depending upon your natural ability, the coach can encourage attempts at most of them (except the firing shot). A good coach is careful to encourage and praise any genuinely good bowling, and to make it clear that if a beginner does not bowl so well, he is not failing, as this is part of the learning process.

SESSION 3

You place the mat correctly and continue with practising the shots you learned during the second session. The coach will again watch each delivery most carefully because this is the important period when

Fig 24   The 6ft long stick to assist correct placing of the mat.

the 'grooving-in' takes place. The practice should continue until you demonstrate a fairly good knowledge of the pace of the green and the line necessary for the playing of a successful shot.

The coach can now describe the firing shot and point out the advantages of playing the shot well and also the disadvantages of too hasty a decision to use the shot as a first option. The exercise with which you are already familiar is set up, of a jack centred at three-quarter length and two bowls at jack-high, close enough not to allow the beginner's bowl to pass through. The coach will watch the early attempts carefully, and explain that each bowler has an optimum weight, pace or speed which they use to drive or fire successfully. This has to be learned by each individual bowler and therefore needs to be practised diligently.

Points regarding the laws of the game (for example, the minimum and maximum distance allowed for jack placing) can be dealt with as they arise naturally throughout the sessions: the beginner need not endure a long lecture on them during the sessions. But the coach may at the end of this session just question the beginner as what he has learned already, and suggest he purchases the booklet on the laws of the game, which they can then spend some time studying together.

SESSION 4

Now you can be introduced to singles, pairs, triples, or fours (rink games), depending upon the availability of co-operative club members. The coach should have already outlined the duties of each player to you, as well as explaining any points of etiquette in the game.

Measuring

Into this session the coach can introduce measuring exercises. You are asked to make an 'eye' judgement as to which bowl is shot. Then you are shown how a measure is used, and invited to try it for yourself. It would be acceptable that if more difficult measuring, i.e. a jack in the ditch, did not arise as a result of play, at the completion of an end, the coach manufactures such a situation, in order that the bowler can learn more about the different types of measure that need to be employed under given circumstances, and how to use them correctly.

The Positions

It could be advisable at this stage, especially in the rink game, for you to have some experience of all positions, and play a few ends at lead, second, third and skip. These are described in full in Chapter 3. This would allow you a better opportunity for playing a fuller range of shots. It will also assist you in being more involved in discussion as to selection of shot, and introduce you to some of the tactics used.

These four sessions will form the basis of sound preparation for any beginner but it is important to remember that the number of these initial sessions can vary, according to the degree of natural ability the new bowler has to offer. A good coach will tailor his coaching sessions to the particular bowler, although this does make coaching more difficult, since no one model for approach or delivery action is imposed. The bowler has also to make quite an input into these early lessons, particularly as he will be encouraged, at all times, to think for himself and to make decisions.

Taking Up the Game

By the end of the initial sessions, the beginner should have developed his own error-free delivery action. He will have learned the importance of finding good line and length, and will have acquired a working knowledge of the laws of the game. Above all, he will have discovered that the game of bowls is played for enjoyment.

3 The Positions in the Game

THE SKIP

First of all, the skips introduce their players to their opponents, which is followed by handshakes all round. The skips then toss a coin to see which side is to play first. Generally two trial ends will be played with two bowls each so that each player should gain some knowledge of the rink. The skip is completely in charge of the rink. He begins to build a head from the moment he decides at what length the jack should be. From then on he will direct play, endeavouring to be flexible in his thinking and planning so as to try to cover all contingencies.

He needs to have a thorough knowledge of the strengths and weaknesses of all his players. He must motivate his players into playing for each other and weld his rink into a formidable unit. He must be many different things to the various players but, above all, he must direct and instruct in such a way that his players have complete confidence in him. As well as being a skilful player, he needs to have a thorough knowledge of the game. Having taken into consideration all the options available, his judgement of the shot to be played must be as accurate as possible and this must be conveyed to his players with confidence.

The skip must always exercise strict self-discipline, even in the face of some poor shots from his players or some very lucky shots from his opponents. A good skip can also be a good coach during any game in so far as he attempts at all times to get the best possible performance from his players. A skip must lead by example and be constructive in his comments in the event of a badly played shot, and enthusiastic in praise of a shot perfectly executed. Therefore, the role of the skip is an extensive one and depends as much on the skip as a person as it does on his ability as a bowler.

THE LEAD

The lead will place the mat for the first end and will ensure it is placed lengthwise on the centre line of the rink. The lead will then deliver the jack to a point where his skip is standing because it is the skip who determines what length may be best for his rink. But the distance the jack needs to travel from the front edge of the mat, to be correctly delivered, is laid down in the laws of the game.

Having delivered the jack to the required distance, the lead will then direct the skip to centre the jack, using the centre pegs as a guide. These are usually numbered and placed directly in line at opposite ends of the rink.

The lead is now ready to deliver the first bowl of the end. His opposing lead will then deliver his first bowl, and each delivers his second bowl in turn. The lead has the responsibility of delivering his two bowls as close to the jack as possible. This will provide his skip with a good foundation for

The Positions in the Game

Fig 25   *The skip providing good guidance to one of his players.*

building the head. Therefore, a good lead needs to be able to bowl a jack consistently well to desired lengths, and be able to gauge the line and length required to draw accurately to any position requested by his skip.

THE SECOND

The second is a key player in any rink game. He must have a variety of shots which he can perform well. If the lead has failed in his task, the skip will usually expect the second to gain the shot. This could be achieved in a variety of ways according to the instructions issued by the skip. If the lead has done well, the second is some-

times expected by the skip to consolidate the position of the head; therefore it is important that the second be proficient in the execution of a wide range of shots.

Before play begins, the second should check that the names of all the players have been correctly entered on the score-card, as this is his responsibility. He must then keep a careful end-by-end record of shots scored – for and against. He will need to check frequently with his opposing second that the scores entered on both their cards are accurate, and he may also be asked to update the score-board. At the end of the game, he may have to make a final check that both score-cards are identical before finally adjusting the score-board and handing the card to his skip.

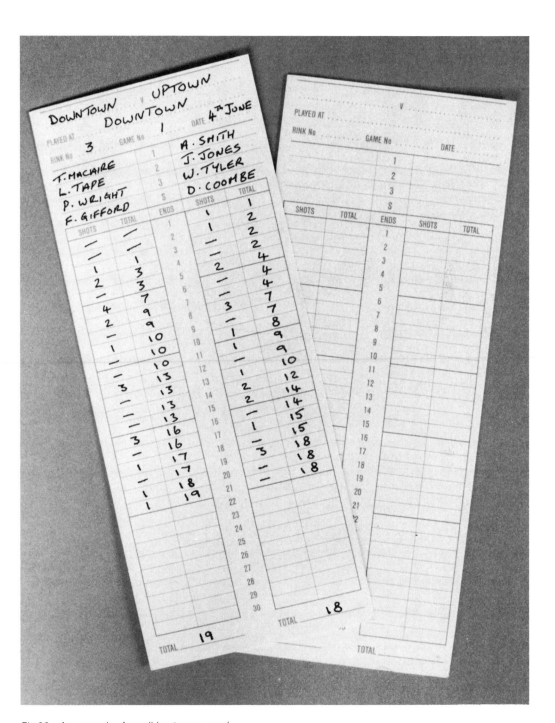

Fig 26   An example of a well-kept score-card.

The Positions in the Game

THE THIRD

The third will usually be at the head with his skip during the time the leads and seconds take to deliver their bowls. He will have seen the head build up from the first bowl delivered and, depending upon the condition of the head, whether favourable or otherwise, he will decide with the skip the selection of shot he will be about to play. He must have at his disposal a wide variety of shots because there will be by now eight bowls in the head, some of which could be a help and others a hindrance.

Good rapport between skip and third is a very important ingredient for a successful four but the skip's decision is final. It is important that skip and third have confidence in each other's judgement, in order that once a decision has been made the third will play his first bowl with confidence and not be in two minds what to do.

Having played his two bowls, the third now returns to the head. The skip may wish to confer with him but, if not, the third will allow the skip to play the shot that the skip himself has selected without further interference. It can be most distracting if a third decides to say something just when his skip is ready to bowl. Therefore, this is not good practice.

When the last bowl of the end has come to rest, the third must agree with his opposing third as to the number of shots – for and against. Sometimes the decision will require the use of a measuring device. The third should be well acquainted with a variety of measures and know how to use them correctly. If the thirds cannot agree, they could invite the skips to measure. If there is still a doubt, the skips will call for an umpire whose decision is final.

Under certain circumstances, the third may be called upon to accept the responsibility of skipping the rink, for example, if the skip is taken ill during the game. He should have prepared himself for such eventualities by having already thought about and studied the qualities necessary for a good skip.

POSITIONAL PRACTICE

Each position in a rink of four is important, and each player needs to know the full range of shots that he could be asked to play at any time, so that he can make as full a contribution as possible.

The Lead

Many would say the lead is a specialized position, demanding consistently good drawing shots. In any end, the early bowls can begin to shape the head; therefore, as with all codes of bowls, the first bowl is so important. A straightforward but purposeful practice could be as follows (*see* Fig 27). Place four jacks on the centre line from minimum to maximum length as dictated by the laws of the game. Beginning with jack 1, and using the forehand only, draw to each jack in turn. Repeat on the backhand. Repeat the exercise, but this time begin with jack 4. This is a good practice for line and length control.

To increase slightly the difficulty of the practice, leave jack 1 in its original position, then move jacks 2, 3 and 4 a little off the centre line, either to the right or left (on the assumption that your opponent may have moved the jack) so that you have to find a slightly different line in order to draw the shot.

Some bowlers dislike seeing an opponent's bowl coming to rest in front of the jack. A lead can be faced with this when his opponent has delivered a very good first bowl. The shot to be played is still a draw to the jack. In practice, you can begin by placing a bowl some 2ft (0.6m) directly in front of the jack and then, by degrees, placing it closer and closer to the jack so that the exercise increases in difficulty and makes greater demands upon your skills as a good drawing bowler.

Equally, there are those who dislike seeing an opponent's bowl coming to rest just behind the jack. As in the practice above, place the bowl 2ft (0.6m) directly behind the jack at first, then bring it closer in stages, until both jack and bowl are touching each other. In both instances, whenever an opponent has delivered a very good first bowl, it is up to you to try to wrest the advantage away from him by playing a bowl of excellent quality.

The lead who has played two very good bowls for his rink, so that the head is building in their favour, can be well pleased with his work. The confidence to play such shots can be bolstered by sound, purposeful practice.

The Second

Before the second plays, four bowls will already have been delivered and, depending upon their position at the head, the second may be asked to retrieve or consolidate the situation. The skip could say, 'Draw the shot' or 'Give me a good second bowl'. The permutations of positions at the head would be far too numerous to include here but we can look at some examples.

In Fig 28, the practice for the second needs to be disciplined to drawing to the jack, either on the forehand or backhand,

Fig 27 An added practice would be for the lead to attempt to deliver each jack to a required distance.

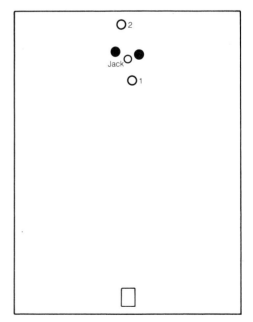

Fig 28 Always practise those situations that cause you most concern.

25

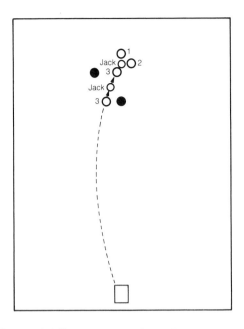

Fig 29   A deliberate drawing of a bowl
through the position occupied by the jack to
a point just beyond, taking the jack with you.

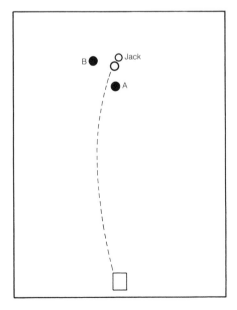

Fig 30   A practice of drawing to the jack,
avoiding all contact with bowls A or B.

since the lead has not contributed very much at all with bowls 1 and 2.

Fig 29 is an example of a situation that could be a good practice for the trail shot, where the second is to bowl on the backhand, with sufficient pace or weight to move the jack to bowls 1 and 2. This shot, correctly executed, could mean the difference from being two shots down to being three shots up, and can have quite a morale-sapping effect upon the opponents.

The second must have mastered a wide variety of shots if he is to make his contribution in full. It is doubtful that there would be many occasions where he would be asked to fire or drive, but a good second should have practised the different types of shot listed earlier, so that if he is asked to play them, he can do so with confidence.

The Third

Depending upon the positioning of the eight bowls already delivered, the third could be asked to consolidate, retrieve, insure, protect, or even, by using a bowl of sufficient pace, break up the head to clear bowls that form some obstruction. It is not entirely correct to think that a third will need to use shots delivered with increased pace to the exclusion of other shots. The game is still essentially a drawing game, and this is the type of shot that the third will be called upon to use more than any other, to whatever position on the green the skip believes will be of the greatest advantage to his rink.

In a practice session, the third can determine which particular shot he is going to play. By careful positioning of bowls, bowled by his own rink and those of the opposing rink, he can arrive at many different positions. For example, if he has made up his mind that he is going to practise drawing to the jack, then Fig 30 would be a good set-up. Begin by placing the opponents' bowls, A and B, at an angle on the backhand so that the drawing shot to the jack must travel between them. By retaining the same angle, as much as possible, bring A and B closer together so that there is less room for the bowl to find its way to the jack, if it is to avoid making contact with either bowl.

Other areas of practice for the third could be the promotion shot where, by making correct contact with a bowl played by his lead or second, he can promote it into a better position or even get the shot (*see* page 33).

It must be remembered that those shots played with increased weight are not exclusive to a third but, in all probability, he will need to play them more than the lead or second. On some occasions he may be asked to play a drive or firing shot, and so it is important that he can do this with confidence. He will have discussed this thoroughly with his skip before executing it and they will also have talked about what could happen to the head if the shot is either perfectly played or not played all that well.

The Skip

It is recognized that the skip must be master of all the shots, as well as variations upon these, some of which may never have been previously seen or heard of. With twelve bowls already having been played, of which some will perhaps be a help to the skip, others a definite hindrance, the skip needs to be brave without being foolish in selecting the shot to be played. There would be less pressure on a skip to play a good drawing shot if his rink was already holding several shots, than if the position were reversed. In some situations the skip might have to play a firing shot, to drive the jack out of the confines of the rink and make it a 'dead end', which must be replayed, thereby giving his rink a chance to win the game. Alternatively, the situation could demand a very accurate drawing shot to the jack, but without moving the jack, as this might give the shot to his opponents.

Despite all types of pressure, the skip is expected to bowl consistently well, either to reinforce his rink's dominance or to retrieve a situation that has gone against him. Therefore, since no two heads of bowls are ever exactly the same, the number of practices that skips could undertake to work at must be legion, and far too many to mention here. Given that a skip is well versed in playing the range of shots required in the game, then he has the important task of deciding on the shot that should be played.

The Selection of Shot

Opinions will vary and arguments rage about this particular aspect of the game. The skip may consult with the other members of his rink before he plays the shot and arrive at a decision by a consensus of opinion, or it could be left entirely to the skip to decide. Before the decision is made, great care must be given to calculate all the possible options and percentages available. A decision arrived at in haste, or without correct consideration, could result in handing the advantage to the opposing rink.

There must never be the 'two minds' syndrome when playing this shot. Regardless of all kinds of pressures, the skip must put all other things out of his mind and concentrate solely and absolutely on the shot that has been selected in order to execute it as perfectly as possible.

4 The Shots in the Game

Having played one or two games for your club, you will now have witnessed a number of different shots being played. Naturally, more experienced players execute their shots with a greater measure of confidence than a player would in the early stages of learning the game. You can only gain this confidence by practising, with the aid of a coach, the whole range of shots.

THE DRAW SHOT

This shot is basic to the game of bowls. It can be played on the forehand or backhand but, if it is going to be successful, it has to be played along the correct line and with the correct weight. The target for the draw shot can vary enormously. It need not always be played to the jack. It can be played to another bowl, or to a spot on the green, so that it comes to rest just at the edge of the ditch. There are a number of permutations for the playing of this shot and the bowler who wishes to compete successfully must master this most basic, but most important, area of play.

Before we look at some practices, it must be stressed that a good line to the target is essential, and so it is important to line up the body to face the line you wish the bowl to travel. The back-swing and the following forward-swing of the bowling arm must also be exactly along this line, so taking time to align the body correctly is essential for a well-executed shot. Secondly, there is the need to deliver the bowl with the correct weight. This means that the bowling arm must be brought forward at the correct speed to reach the target.

A good practice would be to place a jack at about three-quarter length on the rink and then bowl all four bowls on the back-hand as near to the jack as possible, then the next four on the forehand. The curved line taken by the bowl to reach its objective will vary according to the playing surface and weather conditions. That is to say, the line will differ on a fast green from how it is on a slow green (see Chapter 6).

A progression from the above practice is for the bowler to send a bowl up the green (no jack or other object is necessary). The bowler needs to have watched carefully the line taken by the first bowl. Then he will endeavour to bowl the second bowl so that it comes into light contact with his first, with the third bowl touching his second delivery and the fourth bowl touching the third.

Sound, purposeful practices such as these are essential for any bowler wishing to improve his standard of play, and the draw shot is the most important shot to master. Having mentioned already that there are several permutations of the draw shot, let us list some of them.

The Trail Shot

You will see from Fig 31 that the bowler wishes to draw on the backhand (for a right-handed player) so that the jack can be moved to point X. The bowler must now deliver with correct line and length so that the bowl comes to rest at point X and, in the process, move the jack there as well.

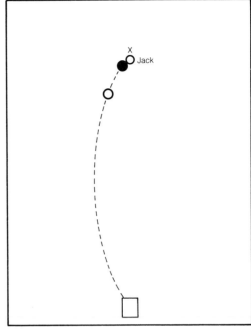

Fig 31 A backhand trail shot used to move jack to point X.

Fig 32 The completion of the trail shot. The jack has been moved to point X.

The weight that must be used is determined by the distance the jack needs to be moved from its original position. Sometimes it needs to be moved no more than a matter of inches but it may be as much as 4ft (1.2m). This is a very demanding shot in terms of skill and accuracy, with the bowler remembering at all times that the shot is still a draw shot and not one to be played with excessive weight. A well-executed trail shot can result in shots against being turned into shots gained (*see* Fig 32).

The Yard On Shot

This shot is exactly what it says. The bowler needs to deliver the bowl so that it comes to rest 1yd (0.9m) beyond a target which could be the jack or another bowl. In some cases, this shot is played with too much weight because a yard on can mean so many different things to so many players. But self-discipline is necessary to play the shot exactly how it should be played, remembering at all times that it is simply a draw shot that is needed.

The Positional Shot

From Fig 33 it can be seen that one player or rink has a collection of bowls at a point behind the jack. To insure against losing shots, the positional bowl can be played so that you draw to the group of opposing bowls. In this shot you are not concerned with the jack but purely drawing to reach a target on the green.

Another variation of this positional shot is to draw to a point on the green where there is no target of bowl or jack. This positioning of the bowl could result in that bowl becoming the shot, should the head and jack be disturbed. This shot is usually played beyond jack-high length and sometimes needs to be bowled around other bowls, so again line and length must be correct.

Ditch Weight

This expression means that the bowl needs to be delivered to a point at the edge of the ditch but ensuring that the bowl is not lost by dropping into the ditch. This is a difficult shot, demanding a high level of concentration and skill. It can come about when the jack has been forced into the ditch so the ditch weight bowl can be the one to gain the shot, or to cut down the shots against (*see* Fig 34).

The Rest Shot

This is where a bowl comes to rest against an opposing bowl (*see* Fig 35). The shot could be played, as mentioned earlier, as a positional shot, or indeed as one to increase your score.

The Wrest Shot

This is when a bowl is played with sufficient weight to dislodge an opponent's bowl so that it takes its place (*see* Fig 36). The degree of dislodgement will depend upon the position of the bowls in the head. The object of this shot is for your bowl to take the place of your opponent's bowl and that if your bowl is delivered with too much weight then this will not happen, so this shot is still essentially a drawing shot.

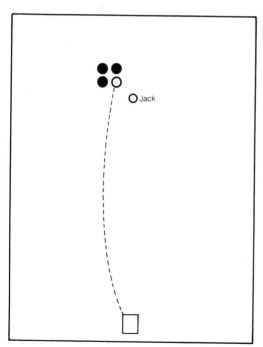

Fig 33   Three back bowls need to be covered in case of the jack being moved to them.

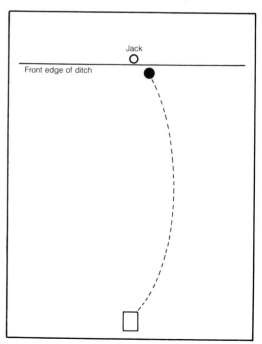

Fig 34   A bowl delivered with ditch weight.

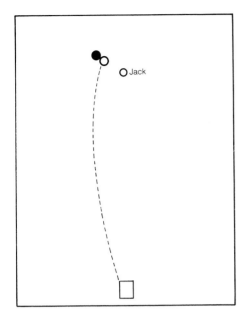

Fig 35   The rest shot.

The Blocking Shot

Arguments abound about the effectiveness of this shot but it is a legitimate tactic which, hopefully, will deny your opponent the opportunity of playing a shot that will disturb a head that is in your favour (*see* Fig 37).

The Wick Shot

This is regarded by some as a lucky shot but it is a perfectly acceptable part of the game. The object is to use the position of a bowl at the head, making a slight contact with it, so that the bowl that is played is deflected, resulting in either gaining the shot or cutting down shots against you (*see* Fig 38). It is still a drawing shot since too violent a contact with the target bowl could cause matters to go badly wrong for you.

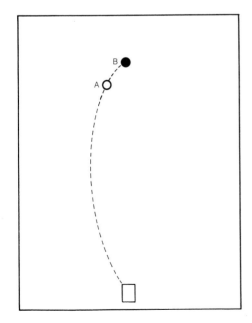

Fig 36   The wrest shot used to move an opponent's bowl from point A to point B, ensuring that your bowl occupies the original position of the opponent's bowl.

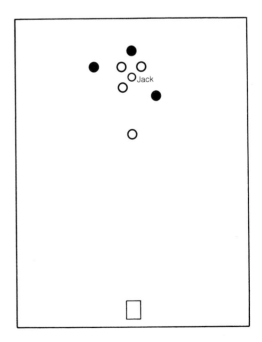

Fig 37   The blocking shot.

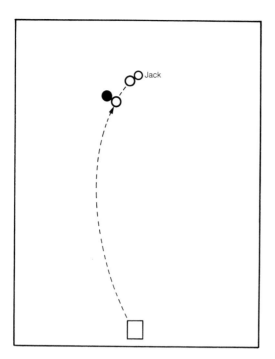

Fig 38   The wick shot.

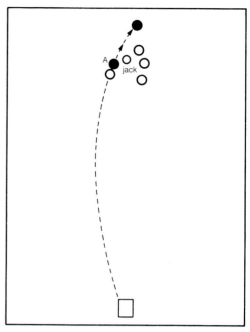

Fig 39   The take out shot used to remove bowl A from the head.

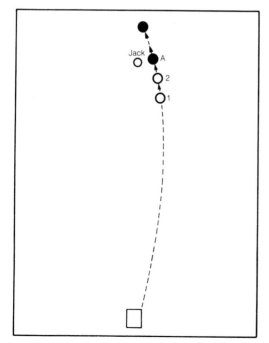

Fig 40   The plant shot.

The Take Out

There could be occasions when an opponent's bowl needs to be removed from the head, resulting in an increased number of shots in your favour. The position in the head of the opposing bowl will sometimes dictate that you bowl with more weight or pace than would normally be necessary for a drawing shot. The faster your bowl travels along the green, the longer the bowl will travel straight. In other words, increased speed or weight can cancel out the normal bias action of the bowl. Therefore, to play a faster bowl means finding a narrower line.

The Plant Shot

This is where bowl 2 is struck with sufficient force by bowl 1 to move it on to bowl A, resulting in bowl A being removed from the head, so that it is no longer the shot or counts in any way (*see* Fig 40).

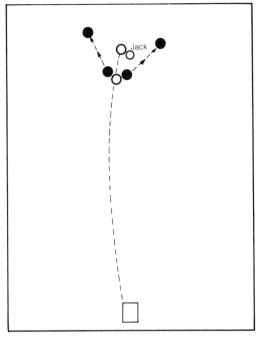

Fig 41   Split shot.

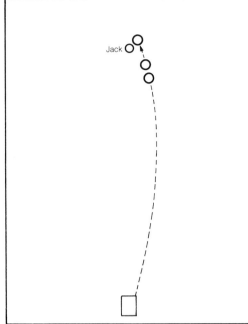

Fig 42   The promotion shot.

The Split Shot

This is where the bowl is delivered along the correct line and with exact weight to dislodge the opponents' two bowls and allow your bowl, the speed of which has been reduced by a contact with the other bowls, to come to rest near the jack.

The Promotion Shot

This is a shot played with sufficient pace to push in one of your own bowls either to reduce the score against you or, hopefully, to get the shot (see Fig 42).

All these variations on the drawing shot demand control, discipline and concentration on finding the correct line and length. Do not wait to be faced with these demanding shots during the course of any game but prepare yourself with practice, practice and more practice so that you can build up your confidence in your ability to play them, whenever the need arises.

Having mastered all the variations of the drawing shot, our bowler can move on to somewhat more demanding skills. These can be deliveries that are played with sufficient pace or weight either to save a situation or destroy a head that has built up against you.

THE OPENING UP SHOT

A shot played with sufficient speed to clear away bowls that have come to rest between the bowler and the jack (see Fig 43). This shot is intended to clear any obstruction so as to allow the bowler a greater number of options for his next bowl.

There are variations of this shot, as indeed there are with the draw shot, but the important point to remember is that they are all played with controlled weight and not

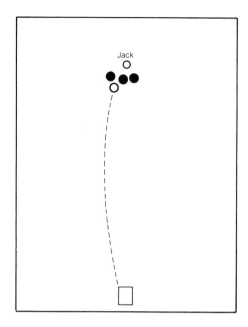

Jack

Fig 43   The opening up shot.

just flung up the green in the hope that something will happen.

THE DRIVE OR FIRING SHOT

This may look exciting or dramatic but it is the shot that must be most carefully calculated because a badly executed drive can be catastrophic. Some bowlers change their stance upon the mat to play this shot but, whatever the stance, be absolutely certain about the speed at which you wish to deliver the bowl as well as the line. The arguments have long gone on as to whether speed or accuracy is most important. It would be best to have both in exact proportion to achieve the perfect result. To drive the jack into the ditch would not demand the bowl to be delivered with the pace you would need to scatter bowls and jack so as to kill the end.

The drive, or firing shot, is a legitimate shot, and should be in the armoury of any bowler who wishes to be able to play the full range of shots available to him. What is important is to be clear about when you feel you should use it. Is it to be a first or last option? Consider this carefully but, having made up your mind, do play it confidently.

It is important to remember that in the playing of this shot most bowlers impart a considerable amount of body weight in a forward direction at the moment they release the bowl. This extra weight must be carefully controlled so that there is no loss of balance and so the bowling arm can come through in an exact line and with the exact speed. One general observation would be that some bowlers increase the length of their forward stride too much – resulting in a loss of balance as the body weight is transferred forward, and also a poorly delivered bowl. So all physical movements must be disciplined and controlled, especially when you drive or fire at your optimum pace. A good drive can achieve advantages other than killing the end; it can be used to reduce the score against you by playing into a group of your opponents' bowls, driving some of them out of the head, and also to drive out an opponent's bowl that is preventing you from picking up a useful number of shots. However, always be careful not to remove any of your own bowls and give the advantage to your opponents.

Driving or firing has brought about some bizarre results, such as driving the jack on to a back bowl with the collision causing the jack to travel back along the green, perhaps resulting in you dropping several shots. Therefore, be sure you have considered everything that could happen. A drive perfectly executed can change the course of a game in your favour but, more than any other shot, it needs to be played with absolute control.

5 Singles, Pairs, Triples and Fours

SINGLES

As there is just you and your opponent, all decisions are your own; there is no one to suggest, encourage or guide you. This one-to-one situation is often preferred by many bowlers but, of course, pairs, triples and fours all have their own excitement to offer.

The object is to bowl as many as poss-ible of your four bowls so that they come to rest in a scoring position. Your opponent will be doing exactly the same so, essentially, the game of singles is a drawing game. Of course, there could be occasions when a heavier bowl needs to be delivered, or even a firing shot or drive needs to be employed. However, think well before us-ing such shots – not only must the decision be correct, but the execution also. Poor

Fig 44   The first bowl is so important.

Fig 45 Who holds the shot?

execution could leave you with a heavy score against, so sum up the situation carefully before making such a decision.

It is important to 'read' the green as soon as possible. Is it fast, medium or slow? Does it offer a good draw? Is one side narrower than the other? All such information is important, to enable you to play to the best of your ability. A hand that proves to be difficult needs to be avoided whenever possible. The vagaries of such a hand or side can have a poor result even when you think you did everything correctly. Beside which, such a shot can have a depressing effect upon your morale and confidence.

As well as 'reading' the green, it is important to 'read' your opponent. Look for any

Fig 46 The umpire measuring to decide which is shot bowl.

weaknesses he may reveal, and be prepared to exploit them whenever you have the opportunity. Do not be overawed by an opponent who may resort to playing heavy shots, and possibly destroy a good head that you have built in your favour by some consistently good bowling. He may not always hit the target and you must be determined to continue to draw to your objective.

At all times, it is important to think of keeping down the score of your opponent by bowling for a good second bowl or shot. It may not always be possible to gain the shot, so discipline yourself not to throw away more shots, but bowl that good second bowl.

There could be occasions when you are holding one shot with a front toucher, and your opponent two or more second shots quite close to the jack (*see* Fig 48). Think carefully before you bowl your last bowl, as a small margin of error on your part could result in you presenting your opponent with two or more shots. Conversely, if your opponent is holding shot and you a good second but the remainder of his bowls are in such a position that the slightest movement of the jack could result in his increasing his score, then you could let him have the one shot and elect not to play your last bowl (*see* Fig 49).

Some players in a singles game make use of the mat. That is to say, they move the mat, within the limits provided by the laws of the game, in the hope that they will disturb the rhythm of their opponent's bowling. This ploy can also be used in pairs, triples and fours. However, the most important skill that you now need to use is delivering the jack. There would be no point in moving the mat well up the green if, when you deliver the jack, it ends up in the ditch. Rolling the jack is such an important skill that aspiring singles players should prac-

Fig 47   This looks to be a good line.

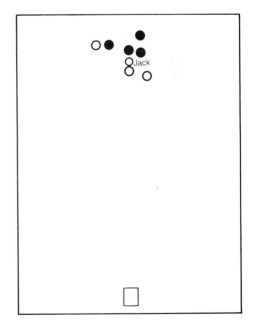

Fig 48   Think well – be content with one shot.

Singles, Pairs, Triples and Fours

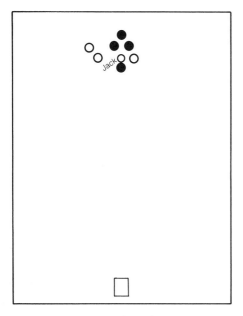

Fig 49   *Let your opponent have the one shot.*

tise it frequently. After all, you are seeking an advantage over your opponent by dictating the length of the jack, so make sure you can bowl it consistently well.

The old adage that 'a game is never lost until it's won' is worth remembering. If your opponent does begin to score well against you, be determined not to give in but keep 'plugging away'. A good result on one end can begin to swing the game your way. Equally important is to remember not to relax if the score is well in your favour. Keep your concentration with every delivery.

Usually, the game of singles will have a marker. He is there to provide you with information but remember that you are allowed to visit the head and see the situation for yourself. This is far better than trying to visualize it when standing some 30yd (27.4m) away. The juxtaposition of bowls in the head can appear to be quite different

Fig 50   *I will try it from here.*

Fig 51   Keep your concentration.

Singles, Pairs, Triples and Fours

Fig 52   The marker is asked to inform the player if the mat is correctly placed.

from a distance. Make sure you acquaint yourself with the real picture before you bowl, because you must carry this image mentally, as it forms part of the necessary information required to play a successful shot.

Take into careful consideration all the options before electing to play a shot. Try to work out what could be the result of using the shot you might want to play. Bowlers describe this as working out the 'percentages'. If you do not weigh up the situation carefully, it could result in your giving away the shot. This will certainly bolster your opponent and could have quite the opposite effect on you. It sometimes demands courage to play a potentially risky shot but, if the state of the game is such that this kind of ploy is called for, it must be played with confidence and not foreboding. Be positive in your approach.

A game of singles can sometimes change dramatically as a result of a fluke. Both players know it was a fluke but if it happens against you, then accept it. No good will came from bemoaning the result. It has already happened. You must now concentrate on the bowl in your hand and not allow the fluke to dominate your approach or attitude.

Of course, the bowler who bowls the most scoring bowls will win the game but sometimes it is necessary to bowl a covering or 'insurance' bowl, especially when your opponent has some back bowls that could be converted into shots or counting bowls. Again, remember not to allow your opponent the luxury of a big score. Study the position of his bowls and provide yourself with some cover, if you think necessary. Try to avoid the situation of having just one bowl in the head. The removal of that bowl could lose you the end, and possibly the game. Make sure always that you have your own fair share of bowls in the head. Never be happy with just one.

In the game of singles, never let the reputation of your opponent cloud your positive thinking. Reputations, after all, were established in the past. You are concerned with the immediate future. It is what happens during your game that really matters. Be firm, and determined to give of your best, and if, on that occasion, your best is not good enough, then recognize the skill of your opponent and accept defeat gracefully. Even the greatest have lost in a game of singles, but they can soon put that defeat behind them and gather themselves for the next game. You must learn to do likewise; there will come another time. We all enjoy winning but even a loser can make a contribution to the game when it is played in the true spirit of sportsmanship, and this, in itself, should be cause for enjoyment.

PAIRS

As soon as you become a player in a pairs game (or triples or fours), then the demands made upon you differ from those for the game of singles. Your contribution to the game as a whole will necessitate more than just bowling skills.

Each pair has four bowls and is made up of the lead and the skip. They play for twenty-one ends. The lead, after delivering his four bowls, will have to assume the role of reading the head as it continues to build, or change, and feed back important information and possibly guidance, to the skip. The lead will have to learn to be aware of any pitfalls, and have a thorough knowledge of the bowling ability of his skip, as

well as understanding the temperament of his partner. Equally, the skip will have to know these facts about his lead. Therefore, as in any team game, there must be compatibility. In the majority of competitions, two bowlers can agree to play as a pair, mainly because of their level of skill, but often because they know they can play well together. They get on with each other off the green as well as on the green. They know they are compatible and this knowledge serves only to strengthen their potential as a difficult pair to beat. Each must have complete confidence in the other. Before a decisive or important shot is to be played, they will often confer quietly, and may reach a consensus decision. But if they differ slightly, it is important that the lead supports the skip in what he decides to do.

TRIPLES

For this game, three players compete against another team of three, each using three bowls and playing for a period of eighteen ends. The order of play is lead, second and then skip.

FOURS

This is also known as a rink of players and involves two teams of four, each using two bowls and playing for twenty-one ends. The order of play is lead, second, third and skip.

In pairs, triples or fours, it is very important that support exists throughout for each player, but not silly support, such as being over-conciliatory when a member of the team has delivered a very poor bowl – and

Singles, Pairs, Triples and Fours

knows it full well – as this can be an embarrassment for that player. Again, this is why it is so important to have a full knowledge of the character and temperament of your team members.

To weld together a good pairs, triples or fours calls for a positive and sensible input from all concerned. Of course, the skip may carry the main task, but all players can make their contribution to the general well-being of the team. It takes just one disruptive element to destroy the compatibility and respect for each other that is necessary to get the best performance from each player.

There could be those occasions when a skip can find himself in charge of a rink where the other three players are complete strangers. This calls for the skip to utilize considerable skills in getting to know his players. He will need to learn the correct form of encouragement, control and guidance he needs to offer each of his players. Of course, the other members of the rink must exercise some 'getting to know you' skills in understanding the skip, so that they can be supportive without being intrusive. Much of the above could be called com-

mon sense but it is surprising how great are the demands made on each player, as well as the responsibilities they must accept in order to play well together.

Some players can always introduce an element of humour into the game. Perhaps it is better to play with a smile rather than a scowl. Others could interpret such humour as a lack of concentration but, generally, a touch of humour can help lift the spirits of the team and, when used carefully and judiciously, can help to relieve any tension that has developed. Therefore, it is important to know when and how to introduce any kind of tactic to raise morale or performance. To bowl well may be sufficient in itself, but there are other qualities necessary to build a really successful playing combination. Some suggestions as to how compatibility can be achieved, within a team, can be found in Chapter 10.

Whatever the game – singles, pairs, triples or fours – always remember that no one should be happy with just one bowl in the head and, when the head is against you, bowling a good second bowl may seem unspectacular, but could be worth its weight in gold.

6 Knowledge of the Green

PACE OF THE GREEN

All the shots mentioned in Chapter 4 must be played bearing in mind the pace of the green. There are, of course, various types that fall between the terms fast and slow green.

Fast Green

This is where the surface is such that it offers minimum friction between it and the bowl. Because of this, a much wider arc or line must be taken by the bowler to allow his bowl to arrive at the target, and this will mean the bowl taking longer to travel the necessary distance (see Fig 54).

Slow Green

This is where the surface provides far greater friction between it and the bowl, thereby making the line much narrower than for a fast green, resulting in the bowl reaching its target in far less time. Usually the speed, or pace, of the green is judged over 30yd (27.5m), as illustrated in Fig 53.

READING THE GREEN

It has been mentioned earlier that correct line and length are the components necessary for the execution of a good shot. Therefore, it is important that the bowler

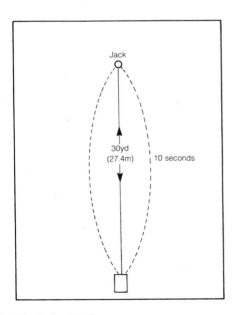

Fig 53   A slow green.

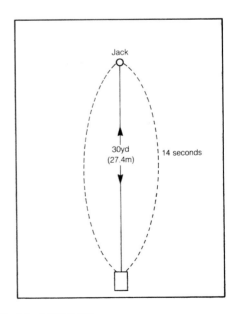

Fig 54   A fast green.

learns to read the green as quickly and as accurately as possible. No bowler can afford to waste the two trial ends which precede the beginning of a game. Use them to the full and concentrate very hard on finding the line and length necessary to achieve a good shot.

It can happen that the playing surface can change during a game. A heavy shower of rain can cause the green to play slower or, conversely, strong sunshine can cause the green to speed up. Therefore, there could be the need for readjustment of line and length during the game, and the adjustment has to be accurate if the bowler is to remain successful. Apart from obvious fast or slow surfaces, a green can vary from rink to rink. For example, at the ends of rinks there are sometimes bare patches where the bowl tends to pick up a little speed. The bowler must build this fact into his 'computer', if he has to bowl over such an area, and make a correction to the speed of his delivery. Such a correction could be minimal, and more often the minimal correction is the most difficult to achieve.

Some rinks have a 'straight run' where the bowl seems to travel in a straight line for a longer distance than usual. It is essential that the bowler learns to make the best of such eccentricities of the playing surface, and not just 'give in' and blame the state of the green. Indoor or outdoor, there are probably very few perfect surfaces and all bowlers need to be determined to bowl at their very best in spite of the vagaries of the playing surfaces.

The tiny differences from green to green, or from rink to rink, are far too numerous to be included here but watch out for them, be aware of them, and above all be determined to conquer them whenever at all possible.

WEATHER CONDITIONS

Strong sunshine and heavy rain have already been mentioned in terms of their effect upon the playing surface. When playing outdoors, it is advisable to adopt the 'be prepared' slogan. Check the contents of your bowling bag thoroughly. See to it that you have the necessary bits and pieces you think are important because a game begun in sunshine can end in wet conditions. The guiding principle must be personal comfort. It is probable that you will not play at your best if you are suffering any discomfort, either from getting a soaking from heavy rain, or getting cold during an evening match. Sensible preparation and the inclusion of suitable equipment can mean the difference between winning or losing the game.

Weather Conditions Affecting Play

A strong wind blowing across the line taken by the bowl can have quite different effects upon the hand (forehand or backhand) that you may choose to play. A bowl can be held up and run further in a straight line before the bias takes some effect or, conversely, be swept inwards at a somewhat accelerated rate towards the head. Line and length need to be carefully 'computed' prior to delivery.

There could be a slight depression which, following rain, could be wetter than other places on the green. This wet patch could cause the bowl to slow slightly so an adjustment of weight or pace must be made. Shadows (from a pavilion, for example) could cause one section of a green to dry more slowly. If it is necessary to bowl across this area, allow for the bowl slowing down a little more quickly as it reaches the damper section and adjust your pace accordingly.

IMAGERY

When playing under pressure and then performing the shot well, some bowlers will admit to having been able to 'see' the shot. That is to say that, from the moment of delivery, they could visualize clearly the path taken by the bowl along the correct line and with the correct weight to arrive at precisely the position required. Some players will walk slowly backwards down the green, keeping a clear mental picture of the head. They may even be reluctant to drop their eyes when picking up the bowl, as the image must remain crystal clear. The alignment of the body needs to be correct for the line selected to the 'target'. It is necessary to visualize the path the bowl will need to take to arrive at a precise spot on the green and then deliver the bowl with exactly the correct weight. Most bowlers will play a more accurate and telling shot if they can employ this positive imagery. Golfers use it when putting. The American golfing expression, 'You drive for show – and putt for dough', was never more true. The golfer on the putting green must 'see' the line the ball takes to the hole. Similarly the snooker player must 'see' this when he plays.

Whatever propels the ball – be it club, cue or hand – it is 'seeing' the line to the objective that is very important, and the bowler will have to concentrate such imagery over a longer distance than the golfer or the snooker player. Some bowlers, having played a shot and walked to the head, may be dismayed to find that the mental picture they had was incorrect. Of course, they could have requested information but this really demonstrates the need to develop one's ability to 'see' more clearly.

7 Preparation for Playing

Bowls can be a very sociable game but even in clubs where people gather for an enjoyable afternoon 'roll-up', the score is still religiously kept. Therefore, the element of competitive play is ever present.

Top players possess, as indeed is the case in all sports, an enormous amount of natural ability but there are also other factors that they must bring in to competitive play.

MENTAL PREPARATION

Sports psychology is not new but more is heard of it today than ever before. It could be considered that as bowls appears to be such an easy game in the physical sense, there is no real need for any kind of mental preparation. Yet most of us have at one time or another played a game well above our usual standard, so if we could isolate all the conditions and circumstances that led us to play so well, then perhaps we could repeat that performance again and again. Some of the factors that contributed to that excellent game could be intensely personal, springing from a sense of well-being, of feeling that everything is going right. However, if bowlers wish to be very competitive, it cannot be left to chance or some haphazard collection of circumstances for them to be correctly mentally prepared for a game.

Athletes can go through a whole routine of personal mental preparation. It is probably a routine devised by the coach and athlete, working closely together over a period of time and eventually arriving at the optimum programme of preparation for that particular athlete.

In meeting with and talking to bowlers, at all levels of the game, it would appear that they are somewhat shy in speaking about their 'programme' of mental preparation. Some will say they do not prepare at all or that they do not wish to think about the game beforehand. However, it appears that most bowlers do have some sort of pattern to follow. No one would go to a game thinking, 'I am going to lose', since there would be no point in going at all. Most bowlers have ploys that they use. Some like to arrive quite early before a game and perhaps take a quiet walk around the green. Others arrive later because they would rather get on with it than 'hang about' before playing.

There are bowlers who will admit to some form of preparation before a game. One bowler, I know, establishes, by carefully polishing his set of bowls, a physical contact that helps to bolster his mental preparation. He is refamiliarizing himself with the feel of the bowls he will soon be using, as he feels that this gives him a greater sense of control and confidence. Some bowlers allow their partners to pack everything they will need for the game, since they rationalize that then they are free to devote all their thinking to the game to be played. Another bowler, prior to the commencement of the game, touches lightly each of his opponent's bowls with his foot. This 'kicking' action, he claims, helps him to establish a mental dominance over his opponent.

The important fact that emerges from these statements is that all the bowlers recognize the need for some kind of preparation. Some may feel that such actions as described above can be of little consequence but, undoubtedly, they form an important part of the mental preparation of the bowlers concerned.

During the playing of a fours or rinks game, a lead may bowl his two bowls and then have to wait perhaps ten minutes before he bowls again. If mental preparation before the game was not positive, then it is possible he will find it very difficult to maintain the concentration necessary for consistently good bowling.

You may still be in the process of finding out the best way to prepare, but you must find it and use it because it will be an important factor in the way you play the game.

Gamesmanship

Thankfully, this is not too evident in the game of bowls but there are some bowlers who might attempt to upset an opponent when that opponent is about to bowl. There is the too loud laugh or noisy conversation; standing almost alongside the bowler who is occupying the mat; and kicking bowls, with the resultant clacking. There are many other ways to distract and those who employ them are perfectly aware of the etiquette necessary on the green; it is not through ignorance that they behave as they

Fig 55   Standing too close behind the player on the mat is not good etiquette.

Fig 56 *Standing alongside the player on the mat is also not good etiquette.*

Fig 57   A too loud conversation can be a distraction to the bowler about to play.

do. It is the responsibility of any bowler to make sure that ideal conditions obtain before he bowls, even if some others have to be reminded of their lack of etiquette and good manners. Do not allow such people to undermine the skills you have to offer or spoil your enjoyment of the game. Remember that when you are ready to bowl, the rink is yours. Make sure that other players understand this clearly. It is always better to make your pointed but polite reminder as soon as you suspect that any form of gamesmanship is being used. Guidelines to good etiquette on the green are laid down in the laws of the game, obtainable from the EBA headquarters (address on page 00). It is the responsibility of every player to be conversant with these guidelines, so that all bowlers can enjoy the game, free from any undue disturbance.

Fig 58   *The noise caused by kicking the bowls can be off-putting for the player in possession of the mat.*

PHYSICAL PREPARATION

Because it would seem that the game of bowls is not physically demanding, some may question the need for any kind of physical preparation. However, it would be well to remember that games can last from two and a half to three hours and, if physical tiredness creeps in, that is sure to affect your mental sharpness.

It has already been mentioned that footwear worn during play must be comfortable, as well as conforming to the laws of the game, since the bowler is standing or walking for the duration of the game.

Some bowlers may have to travel long distances by car to a venue. If you are in this situation, make sure you arrive in time for a gentle or brisk stroll to get rid of any stiffness resulting from the long journey.

Stretching Exercises

Bowls can be played to a grand old age but some bowlers will experience a stiffness in their joints, particularly the knees. Some simple stretching exercises may help.

Fig 59   Any unnecessary movement by players at the head constitutes a distraction for the player about to deliver his bowl.

Knees

Take two kitchen chairs and place them back-to-back, about 18in (45cm) apart. Place a hand on each of the chairs and then, by supporting the body with your hands and arms, place the right foot forward between the chairs. Now gently lower the body (keeping the rear leg as straight as possible) as far as you can comfortably and without strain. This action of lowering and raising the body can be repeated until you are ready to change to the left leg being brought forward. Movement should be controlled and not done in a hasty fashion. This exercise should help to keep the knees more supple.

Wrists

Some bowlers experience a stiffening of the wrist in their bowling arm. Holding the forearm parallel to the floor, just rotate the hand first clockwise and then anticlock-

51

wise. There is no need to tire yourself but a few minutes each day could prevent extra stiffness in the wrists.

Neck, Shoulders and Arms

A quite simple exercise of lowering the chin towards the chest, then turning the head gently to look over the left shoulder, returning to the chest and repeating the exercise to look over the right shoulder, should help to keep the neck supple. For shoulders and arms, the exercise used by swimmers before they enter the water of 'shaking down' from the shoulders to the tips of the fingers can help relieve some tension. There are some bowlers who just 'shake down' their bowling arm and as a result feel that their delivery action is far smoother.

The Back

Just a gentle 'touch the toes', or forward bend as it was once known, can help to make the back a little more supple. Beware of making sudden or jerky movements during this exercise. It needs to be controlled and done slowly, especially when returning to the upright position.

These simple exercises are suggested for those who do not have more serious problems, such as arthritis. They are simply intended for relieving any stiffness that may appear. The regularity and length of time anyone may wish to devote to them is entirely personal.

If you are a sufferer from arthritis in the wrists or knees, then working with a coach for a time could be advantageous. Coaches have rebuilt or redesigned a delivery action for bowlers who have experienced such problems, and a good coach can help you to deliver the bowl as smoothly as possible, so that your enjoyment of the game can be the greater.

Finally, we should not overlook the obvious: walking is an excellent form of exercise and can help to keep muscles toned. A brisk walk is preferable to a stroll. To walk briskly for twenty or thirty minutes is an exercise that is now recognized as having an excellent effect upon groups of muscles. It is not simply a question of age but a question of preparation, a toning and building up of endurance in order that you last through a game without feeling too tired towards the end because, undoubtedly, tiredness will affect your performance.

Preparation Practice

In almost all major sports, practice forms an important part of preparation for perform-

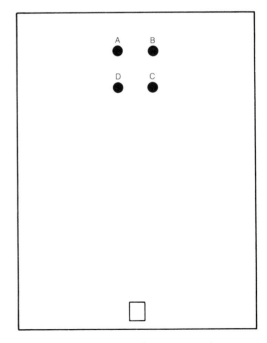

Fig 60   *This situation can offer many sound practices.*

ance. Bowls is a game of great skill and all skills need to be practised. The game of bowls has, because of its exposure on television, recently gained the image of being an exciting and demanding sport, but, in fact, it was ever thus. It really does not matter what level any individual bowler wishes to achieve for practice to be a must. However, it is important that bowlers adopt a disciplined approach to practice and that at all times it remains purposeful.

Example 1

Four bowls are set in a 4 × 4ft (1.2 × 1.2m) square (see Fig 60). The first part of this practice is to bowl so that your bowl comes to rest within the confines of the square, with the bowl entering the square between C and D.

The next stage is enter the square between bowls B and C on the forehand and bowls A and D on the backhand. This is an excellent line and length exercise and, of course, is purely a drawing exercise.

Now draw to each bowl in turn on the forehand, and then to each bowl in turn on the backhand. Play a shot of controlled weight on to A on the forehand so that your bowl just moves A from its position and takes its place. Repeat the exercise to bowl B, using the backhand.

On the forehand, play a promotion shot on to bowl C, so that it is moved as near as possible to the centre spot in the square. Repeat the exercise on the backhand with bowl D as the target bowl.

These represent just a few of the purposeful practices that can be used from the set-up shown in Fig 60. You can nominate your shot and play it with different weight, depending on what you wish to achieve. You can, of course, devise your own form of practice shots to play but, above all, you

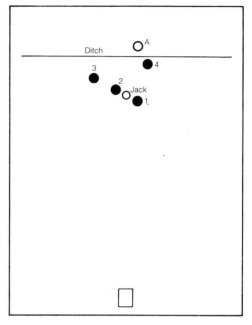

Fig 61 Another practice demanding good line and length.

need to concentrate the practice on those shots which you may not always play with confidence.

Example 2

Draw as close to the jack as possible, by bowling one bowl on the forehand and one on the backhand. With the third bowl, draw as close as possible to the point marked X. Play the fourth bowl with sufficient weight to put bowl A into the ditch, but making sure your bowl stays on the green (see Fig 61).

Various permutations on these suggestions can be employed by the player concerned but one of the attributes of a good player is one who can use extra weight with one bowl and then draw a precise length with the next. Therefore, vary the exercise so that you play the heavier shot first, then draw to the jack.

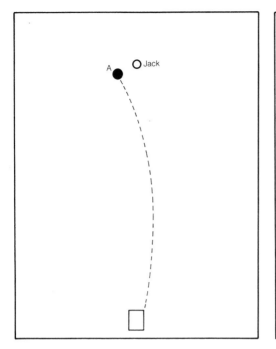

Fig 62   *Bowling to bowl A will require a minimal adjustment in line from that required to bowl to the jack.*

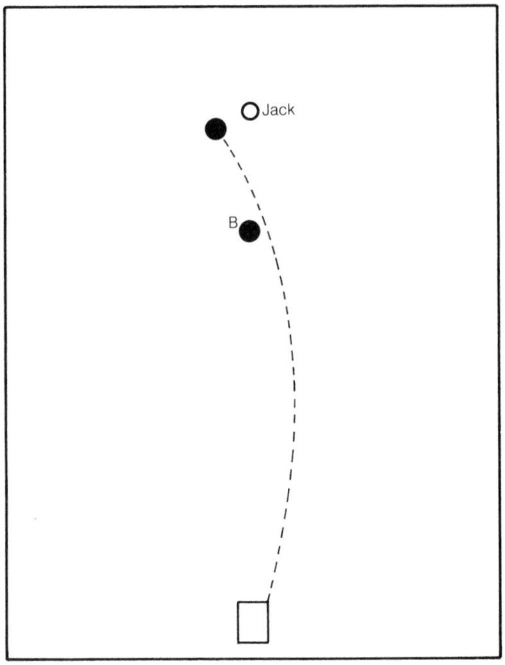

Fig 63   *Bowl B increases slightly the degree of difficulty.*

Bowl A is just short of the jack on the backhand (*see* Fig 62). Practise the shot, using the forehand, just to ease bowl A further away from the jack. By placing bowl B an appropriate distance in front of the jack, and still playing the same kind of shot on the forehand, it will be seen that bowl B is increasing the degree of difficulty of the exercise (*see* Fig 63).

Further bowls can be placed judiciously so that the practice is made more demanding of bowling skills.

8 Club Officials

CAPTAIN

Clubs sometimes elect their captains for reasons other than simply being a good player. A club captain might be playing as a lead, which is a very responsible playing position but not one where he can exercise a great deal of influence during a game, as is the case in some other sports.

It could be that a club captain is concerned with improving the ethos within the club by encouraging good standards of etiquette from club members as well as guiding members to feeling a sense of pride in their membership. He can organize such events as practice evenings, where he selects the rinks which will play against each other, possibly with some reward at the end of the season for the overall best performance. He should be diplomatic in dealing with the occasional grievance but firm in dealing with a member who ignores any of the club rules.

He is usually involved in the selection of teams and, in some instances, finds this a thankless task and one open to criticism, so he must have the courage to justify his opinions. He will be involved in the general running of the club along with the club committee, at which he must be articulate enough to convince others of his aspirations for any improvements that he believes it is necessary to introduce.

Above all, he must lead by example, by being an excellent club member and above reproach because with any title comes responsibility, and his behaviour, in all its aspects, will be closely scrutinized. If it is positive and acceptable, then he can have a direct bearing on the club as a whole and lead to an improvement in the attitudes and standards of the members. He must work hard at making his club such that people would wish to belong to it.

There are, of course, other minor duties that a captain must fulfil but, most importantly, a captain should, at the end of his term of office, be able to look back with some pride at any improvement he has instituted.

MANAGERS AND NON-PLAYING CAPTAINS

Both of these titles are well known in many sports but are relatively new in the game of bowls. People appointed to such positions are expected to provide their teams with that sense of well-being and confidence before a game. The players must be correctly prepared and well motivated in order that they go into the game in the most positive frame of mind that can be induced. The way in which these objectives may be achieved will vary according to the capabilities of the people appointed to such positions. Above all, they must know their players not only as individuals, but also as rinks. They must be aware of the needs of all, since that will determine their pre-match programme of preparation.

Some people in charge of teams may settle for a 'get together' of all the players where the manager can expand on theories or ideas that might achieve the desired effect upon his players. Others will turn to the use of such techniques as showing a video of good previous performances, in the hope that the players will dwell on all the good and positive points they have viewed, and have no negative thoughts about the forthcoming game. Videos also provide the reality of the shouts of encouragement and noise level that generally occurs during such games, especially in indoor matches. For any new player this could come as a surprise and something of a shock. Even a vicarious experience could be better than none, and may help the new player in the team not to be overwhelmed when he does face such things in reality.

Fig 64 The lollipop indicators inform the players of the number of shots for or against.

Other methods are to call upon the National Coaching Team of the English Bowls Coaching Scheme to prepare a weekend of coaching activities, finishing off with a match against a selected team.

Therefore, the role of managers and non-playing captains is to be involved in some form of preparation to help the team play to its fullest potential, and to guide all players in being fully supportive of each other and convince them of their ability to win.

THE MARKER

Any club member can be invited to act as a marker in a game of singles. Obviously the marker must have a sound knowledge of the game of bowls if he is to play his part in full. In the EBA booklet on the laws of the game, there are guide-lines laid down for the marker, and it would be well for anyone to read these before stepping on the green to carry out this duty.

There are some general principles that should be followed. Never volunteer information to either of the players; the marker should only answer a direct question from a player and, in answering, should be as succinct and yet as informative as possible. The marker should never be afraid to admit any uncertainty. If, for example, he is requested to inform a player as to which bowl is the shot, and the proximity of the opponent's bowl is such that he is not sure, he should indicate that he is not able to answer the question without measuring. This, of course, cannot be done until the end is completed. The player who posed the question is at liberty to walk to the head and make his own judgement. There are frequent requests from bowlers to be told the distance between a bowl and, for example, the jack. Of course, the marker must attempt to be as accurate as possible in his answer, but often 'eye judgement' can be up to around 2in (5cm) over or below the actual distance.

The marker needs to adopt a position either to the left or right of the centre line, and behind the jack. During the playing of the end, he must remain as still and unobtrusive as possible. At the conclusion of the end, the marker allows the players to make a collective decision as to how many bowls are scoring bowls. Under no circumstances should he move any of the bowls before the two players arrive at the head. If player A agrees that his opponent has scored two shots, the marker will enter this on the score-card. During the

game, both players need to be regularly informed by the marker as to their individual scores. Even in inclement weather, the marker must make every effort to keep the score-card clean and dry. At the conclusion of the game, he invites both players to sign the score-card and then disposes of the card according to the rules of that particular competition or tournament.

A marker could be invited to measure for shot if the players cannot agree. Directions for measuring are laid down in the EBA rule book but it can be a demanding exercise and it would be advisable for any club member to have had some experience of measuring. A marker obviously needs to carry a measure, but would not have the

Fig 65   Just one of the measures available for use by bowlers.

array of sophisticated measuring apparatus that would be carried by an umpire. If, having completed the measuring, his decision is not acceptable to one or both players, then the marker can call in an umpire, whose decision is final. If no umpire has been appointed for that particular competition, the marker can select one and his decision will equally be final.

Some duties, such as those just mentioned and also the marking of touchers and the removal of 'dead' bowls from the ditch, have all been clearly laid down by the governing body but a good marker can make a positive contribution to the game generally. He must have a sense of purpose as well as a sense of humour and must enforce the rules of the competition fairly and firmly, and never be seen to be prejudiced or biased in any way. His contribution can be heightened by a good standard of general behaviour and correct etiquette, and by presenting to the players a presence that is totally acceptable.

UMPIRES

During the playing of any game, match, tournament or competition, the umpire who has been appointed to serve at the event is there to enforce the laws of the game. His decision is final in any dispute that may arise.

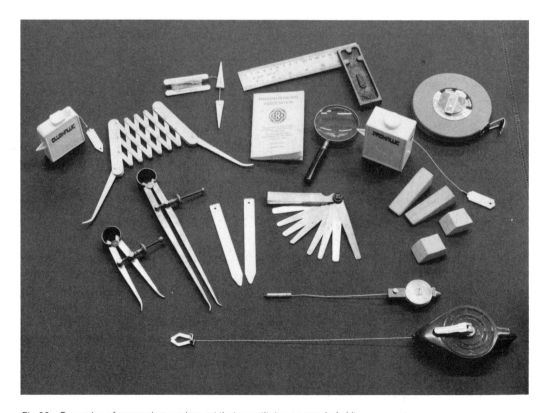

Fig 66   Examples of measuring equipment that constitutes an umpire's kit.

Fig 67   Callipers being used for a close measure.

Fig 68   Feeler gauges.

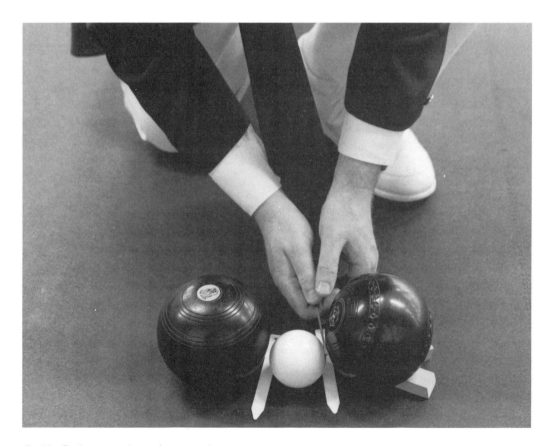

Fig 69   Feeler gauges in use for a very close measure.

Following an examination, players can qualify as umpires. If you want further details, contact:

Norman Deeprose
24 Elm Green Close
Bath Road
Worcester
WR5 3ID

Having qualified and demonstrated a responsible approach to the demands of umpiring, there are many bowlers who are able to offer the game an added dimension. Whenever there are rules or laws, it is necessary to have someone who will interpret them correctly and see to it that they are enforced. Umpires can also contribute to the maintenance of good standards in the game, and encourage the correct spirit in which it should be played.

Measuring

At the completion of an end, the number of shots, for and against, have to be counted. Sometimes it is not possible to tell which is the shot without using a measure. There are

Fig 70   Wedges being used to prevent a bowl from falling over when the bowl it is resting against is removed.

Fig 71   This bowl is out.

Fig 72   This bowl is in.

Fig 73   The Torpedo Measure.

Fig 74   The Torpedo Measure being used when measuring from the ditch
to the playing surface.

Club Officials

many varieties of measure available but, whatever kind is used by players, markers or umpires, great care is needed not to disturb the bowl or jack during the process of measuring.

The umpire, of course, will carry a number of sophisticated measuring devices, as some decisions can border on the hair-line and must be measured with great precision. Callipers can sometimes be employed for fine measuring, but there are situations when a measuring device of a more delicate nature is used, such as a feeler gauge. The umpire must ensure that there is no movement of the bowl, especially when one bowl is leaning on another. Therefore, wedges come into play. The square is employed to determine whether a bowl is in or out of play.

Since some games can be decided on a measure, it is necessary for the umpire to have at his disposal a wide variety of measuring devices in order to cover almost every contingency.

Normally, in a rinks or fours game, decisions as to which bowl is shot will be arrived at and agreed upon by the thirds. If they have any doubts, the skips can be asked to measure. It is not often that an umpire need be called. It is important that players know how to measure correctly and so they should practise this away from the game situation. A bungled attempt at a measure can introduce unnecessary discord into a game, so it is very important to get it right. Guidelines as to the correct method of measuring are usually to be found in the 'Laws of the Game' booklet.

9 Personal Practice

Most players of games have, at some time or other, suffered a falling off in their performance, and those who play bowls are no strangers to this syndrome. Now there are many bowling clubs which have coaches, qualified by the EBCS, established in clubs and ready to work with players at all levels who may seek their advice. Some clubs set aside a number of rinks on a particular evening of the week where time and space are reserved for coaching. If your game is suffering in some way, you can attend such sessions and, with the aid of a coach, may soon be able to put your game together again. It is essential that you state any problems you have honestly.

The coach will watch your technique from the moment the bowl is picked up. The grip employed, the stance on the mat, the back-swing and the delivery will be carefully noted. Correct delivery of the bowl does not simply involve the swinging of the arm in a forward direction and release of the bowl. The whole body is involved, from

Fig 75   An example of the upright stance.

Fig 76   A slight variation on the upright stance.

Fig 77 A more crouched stance.

the tips of the toes to the crown of the head, and it needs only one action to be slightly wrong or awry, for the result to be less than satisfactory.

TECHNIQUE

The Grip

There are many variations in the way a player grips a bowl (see Figs 11,12,13 and 14) and sometimes the coach can help by suggesting some minor change to the grip. Regardless of type of grip, it is important

that the bowl be held in an upright position and not leaning one way or the other, or the result can be a wobbled delivery.

Other factors that will produce a wobble are when the small finger is too high on the side of the bowl, or the thumb, as this is the last part of the hand to touch the bowl at the moment of release.

The Stance

The position of the feet will vary but the most important requirement must be that of perfect balance. If this is not achieved, undue strain is placed upon the bowler,

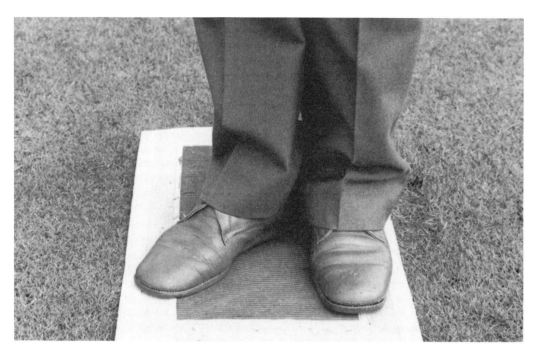

Fig 78   Variation 1: the positioning of the feet when adopting stance.

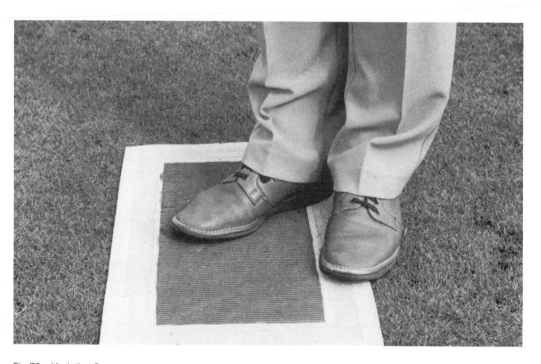

Fig 79   Variation 2.

Fig 80   Variation 3.

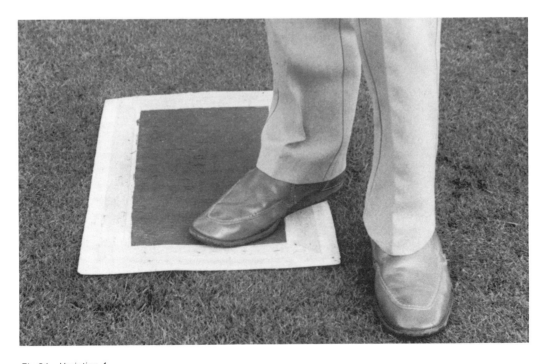

Fig 81   Variation 4.

regardless of whether the stance is upright or crouched.

The Back-Swing

Probably the best way to think of the back-swing is as an even pendulum movement. How far the pendulum travels is entirely the choice of the bowler. What must not happen is for the arm to move outwards and away from the body at the end of the back-swing, nor need the bowl be at the other extreme, tucked behind the body. Both positions will demand adjustments during the forward-swing and can result in a poor delivery. During the back-swing, the bowling arm should be kept as close to the body as possible – in fact, brushing the hip. This provides better overall control and prohibits the bowling arm becoming wayward.

Some bowlers will increase the length of the back-swing if they need to deliver the bowl at greater speed. Others will not alter the length of the back-swing at all, but simply bring the bowling arm forward at an increased pace. There are those who, when they need to play the drive or firing shot, will quicken the pace of the back-swing. This needs to be carefully controlled if it is to be successful.

Some players may have wide hips, which does not assist a free pendulum movement but inclining the body slightly to the right, in the case of a forehand delivery for a right-handed player, can help to cancel out the wider hips, and allow a smooth, uninter-

Fig 82   The twist of the wrist at the end of the back-swing.

Fig 83   A good follow-through action.

rupted back-swing. Generally, when right-handed players play their backhand the alignment of the body does help to eliminate part of the problem caused by wider hips.

During the back-swing, there are some bowlers who twist the wrist outward, so that the back of the hand is closer to the body than is the bowl. It is well known that one of the greatest bowls players of all time, David Bryant CBE, includes such an action in his back-swing. It works for him and is an in-built part of the mechanics of his delivery action. Some bowlers find that this twisting of the wrist does help to keep the bowling arm closer to the body but, before delivering the bowl, the wrist has to be straightened again. This should not present too great a problem but it might be advisable for bowlers to limit movement to a mini-mum, and therefore reduce the number of things that could go wrong.

The Forward-Swing

Often this action is combined with the forward step and the whole of the body moving forward in a controlled manner. With this much movement, it could be the time when things go wrong. The slightest loss of balance can affect the whole of the delivery action. The forward movement of the bowling arm needs to be as smooth and deliberate as possible. Some bowlers speed up the forward action over the last 12–18in (30–45cm) of their delivery. This can result in a bowl being pitched out of the hand.

At the very end of the forward-swing, the fingers should be almost brushing the grass or carpet to prevent the bowl bumping – again we are back to bending the knees sufficiently to achieve that smooth delivery.

It is not good practice for the bowler, at the moment of release, to twist the hand inwards towards the body (that is for the right-handed player playing the forehand). Some believe, mistakenly, that this action assists the bias. What can happen is a wobbled delivery and an unsatisfactory result.

The Follow Through

There are the long and short varieties to this but each should be along the correct line. It is sometimes unwise for players to finish their delivery action by bringing the bowling arm across the body. A good clear follow through helps to concentrate the mind on the whole delivery action, whereas any sideways movement of the arm, if begun a fraction too soon, could bring about a poor result. A good follow through action also helps to concentrate the eyes of the bowler on the line travelled by the bowl. If this is the correct line, it is important to hit it again and again, and this can be helped by a good follow through action.

The Non-Bowling Arm

The important point about the non-bowling arm is that it should be in the same place for each delivery. Some players place their non-bowling hand on their thigh, others may grasp the knee of their leading leg. For those who allow the non-bowling arm to be free, they must be careful to control the amount of movement as well as where the arm should be placed to achieve the best possible balance.

Fig 84   The non-bowling arm is placed firmly on the knee of the leading leg.

Fig 85   *Looking down at the feet at the moment of release can cause the player to lose his line.*

The Position of the Head

Having decided the line along the green that his bowl has to travel and seen this clearly in his mind's eye, the bowler delivers the bowl. But the position of the head is critical at the moment of release. There are some bowlers who look downwards at the moment of release and this can cause them to lose the line. They sometimes release slightly behind the leading foot and before the forward-swing is fully complete. Conversely, there are others who hold the head too high. This puts a strain on the neck and shoulders which can transmit itself to the bowling arm. Also, the delivery can be bumped because the bowling arm

is already moving upwards before the bowl is released.

There is a position that is the most comfortable and profitable for all bowlers, which is that the eyes should be concentrated at a point along the line the bowl is to take. The distance from the mat of this point of eye contact will vary from bowler to bowler. The head must remain still but not rigid, and it is up to every bowler to find that point along the line where the head is held comfortably and without strain, when delivering the bowl.

Many bowlers will opt for looking at the shoulder on the green. That is to say, the point at which the bias begins to work and the bowl to curve towards its objective. Others will select a point only a few yards along the line and concentrate on delivering the bowl so that it travels across that point of aim.

Another head movement that can result in the bowl being pitched out of the hand is when the head is jerked too high and too quickly at the moment of release of the bowl. So it would be well to remember that the head position needs to be relaxed, comfortable and as still as possible.

The Leading Foot

Generally it need be no longer than a walking pace forward, it should provide perfect balance and be pointing along the delivery line.

REMEDIAL PRACTICE

It would need a book in itself to look at each minor or major fault that can creep into anyone's game, but the following cover the main problem areas and the approaches a coach may use to remedy them.

Fig 86   The position of the head is too high to allow a smooth delivery.

Fig 87   Correct positioning of the head allows the bowl to be delivered correctly.

Fig 88   The bowl is bumped because the head has been jerked upwards at the moment of delivery.

Bowling a Good Line

The coach will invite you to pick up the bowl and bowl on the forehand, then repeat the exercise on the backhand. If your problem has only been on the forehand, for example, you might wonder why the coach asks for a bowl to be delivered on the backhand as well. The reasoning is that some bowlers alter their delivery from forehand to backhand without even being aware of this. A good coach may soon pick up one of these small changes and begin to work from there.

The Hooked Bowl

It is easy for bowlers to fall into the trap of lining up by use of the head and eyes only, and forgetting that the whole body should be aligned with the selected line.

The coach may notice that at the moment of release, the left foot (the leading foot for the right-handed bowler), rather than being straight along the required line, has the toe pointing to the right, or the foot may have moved to directly in front of the right foot. Either of these can cause a slight imbalance, which results in the right arm being hooked from right to left at the moment the bowl is released. This hooking action is not conducive to obtaining the correct line.

The coach will invite you to place a strip of white card (or perhaps a cardboard cutout of a foot) on the spot that you believe your left foot should be at the moment of delivery. It is unlikely that you will place the visual aid in exactly the right place but you will probably place it reasonably correctly, with the toe pointing along, and not across, the line. The coach can then suggest that you place your leading foot on the marker at the point that you have indicated, during your delivery action.

The coach will be patient, and not expect spot-on perfection each time, because probably you have been placing your foot wrongly for some time and now have to make quite an adjustment.

When the remedial exercise is done correctly, you will be able to feel, as well as see for yourself, that your delivery arm is no longer hooking across your body, and this will probably result in you bowling a better line.

However, a hooked bowl can also be caused by an incorrect alignment of the body on the mat, or the arm being hooked across the body. The body should be squarely facing the chosen line. If the body is not square to this line but has the leading shoulder pointing along it, the arm will be hooked. We are now using the example of a right-handed player who puts his leading (left shoulder) forward. On the backhand, if the leading shoulder is again in a forward position, the stance is not that comfortable and, on releasing the bowl, the player will often turn his wrist outward, resulting in a poorly delivered bowl.

Finding the Correct Line

It could well be that you have a smooth delivery but are still unable to bowl a consistent line. Therefore, another factor must be the cause of failure.

The coach may pose a very basic question: 'Where do you think the correct line is?' He could even invite you to walk the line along the green. If the line selected by you is inaccurate, the coach will suggest that you work together to find a more correct line. The coach should not impose but simply suggest, because this kind of personal practice must be two-way and never simply the coach issuing a stream of instructions.

Fig 89   The head held too high at the moment of delivery causing the bowl to be bounced when leaving the hand.

If the line chosen and pointed out by you seems reasonably correct, the coach can bring that line closer to you within about 6yd (5.5m) by placing a white handkerchief or thin white card on the green at the selected spot. He then invites you to bowl over the marker. When you have done this satisfactorily for, say, four to six deliveries, the coach takes the marker further away and asks you to repeat the exercise. Now that you have some point of reference, you may experience an improvement in finding the correct line.

The coach will gradually wean you away from the visual aid and put the responsibility for finding the correct line squarely on

your shoulders. Since the coach has demonstrated that there was no major problem preventing you from finding the correct line, this in itself could be sufficient to restore your confidence.

Bowling at the Correct Pace

One aspect of the game of bowls that concerns some bowlers is that of bowling incorrect weight or pace. One of the reasons for this could be an inaccurate reading of the speed of the green (i.e. whether fast or slow) and all players must endeavour to become better at judging this.

There are other factors that can have a bearing. It should be reiterated that the whole of the body is involved in the delivery action, so let us look carefully at some points that can influence the speed at which a bowl is delivered.

The Height of the Stance

Many bowlers, when playing on a fast green, will instinctively lower the whole body nearer to the running surface. This helps to limit the forward pace that the bowler takes and allows him a better feel of the bowl leaving his hand, which could lead to greater control at the moment of release.

Conversely, on a slow green, some bowlers will remain more upright, with the head at an increased height above the green, so that when the step forward is taken, more of the body weight can be imparted to the bowl.

The Length of the Forward Stride

Some bowlers will increase the length of the forward stride to provide more impetus to the bowl but this has to be carefully controlled. Too long a forward stride can result in a bowl being poorly delivered.

The Length of the Back-Swing

Other bowlers will increase the length of the back-swing to offer more propulsion to the bowl. What must be ensured here is that the back-swing is controlled and the bowling arm not allowed to swing away from the body but kept as close to the hip as possible.

The Speed of the Arm

This is one of the most important aspects of good weight control. As with the golfer, the back-swing may be the same but the speed at which the club-head comes through will be tailored to the shot required. Bowlers should think carefully about this aspect of the delivery action. If the arm is brought forward too quickly, it can result in the bowl being too heavy to achieve the objective. Obviously, the arm being brought forward too slowly will result in a short bowl, which is never the favourite result with bowlers.

To achieve good length bowling, the coach will ask you to stand on the mat, without a bowl in your hand. The coach squats down in front of you with his right hand held open, fingers pointing downwards. You go through your delivery action, as though you were bowling to a minimum-length jack. The coach will instruct you to strike his hand with the speed you think necessary to reach minimum length. He will constantly change the length required, forcing you to think continually about speed of the arm coming through.

Bowlers very quickly catch on to this exercise. When the coach next invites you

to pick up a bowl, you will remember what you have already built in to your bowling 'computer' – the speed needed to achieve a particular length. Therefore, now you should be far more conscious of the need for control.

The coach has concentrated your thinking on one small, but very important, area of the delivery action that does more than most other aspects already mentioned, towards bowling with correct weight. Experience has shown that a better and more consistent pace of bowl can generally be achieved by bowlers who have taken part in such an exercise.

It could be that frustration at not being able to bowl the desired weight of bowl has caused you to have 'the harder I try the worse I become' syndrome. By making you concentrate fully on just one aspect of your delivery action, the coach may have helped to overcome this block, which may have been making you tense.

The Bumped Bowl

There are several reasons why this happens. One is if the bowler lunges forward so that the bowl is pitched away and not rolled away. Another is the too long forward stride, where control of body weight is much more difficult and can result in a bumped delivery. A further cause may be that the player is not close enough to the bowling surface and so the result is that the bowl is dropped. This can be overcome by simply bending the knees sufficiently to lower the body before delivery.

It should be emphasized, however, that if your delivery action is different from the text books, this is not necessarily a cause for concern. If it is successful, then leave well alone. Every delivery is individual to the

Personal Practice

Fig 90   An example of the body not having been lowered close enough to the playing surface with the result that the bowl is bumped.

Fig 91   A very personal grip and back-swing.

Fig 92   However, he achieves a very smooth delivery.

Fig 93   A whole body follow through after release of the bowl.

Personal Practice

bowler himself, and the more bowlers that one sees in action, the more evident this fact becomes. Even during the playing of a game, bowlers may need to introduce some minor differences in their delivery action. They may adopt a slightly different stance, depending upon the pace necessary to deliver the bowl. Whatever differences are introduced, though, the bowler must always exercise absolute control over all body movement.

10 The Coach

Before a coach takes a remedial session, he will need to have acquainted himself with a host of minor differences in delivery actions that can bring about a less than fruitful result. Many bowlers may have the same problems, but totally different contributory factors, so the coach has a great deal of preparation to undertake. He will need to have a mental check-list that he can recall as soon as the problem is explained by the bowler. Obviously he will need to have the trust and confidence of the bowler he is trying to assist and, above all, he must possess the skills necessary to establish a rapport with each individual bowler.

The coach must not be dictatorial or dogmatic but rather involve the bowler as much as possible in the remedial stage, not simply standing yards away issuing one instruction after another. Good coaching demands the involvement of both coach and bowler throughout the whole session. A 'them and us' syndrome is not conducive to good coaching or the correction of faults. These statements may seem to be obvious but they are those that coaches need to bear in mind at all times.

Coaching at club level is now well respected because coaches have demonstrated the correct attitude and approach necessary to gain the confidence of bowlers who are experiencing some difficulties. When, after working closely with the bowler, the coach has been able to iron out the kinks that were worrying the player, the reward for him will be simply to see that bowler's increased enjoyment when next he plays.

BOWLS COACHING CLINICS

Many people attend coaching clinics to seek advice and assistance because, in one area or another, they may be experiencing a falling-off in performance. When approached by such a bowler, the coach must begin his 'reading' of the client. He should watch how they move; a lot can be learned from a handshake. Perhaps he will identify an obvious reason for the bowler being unable to deliver a bowl smoothly. Then there follows some discussion time, where the coach will invite the bowler to state what he believes to be the problem. Often the reply is 'I don't know', but the coach must not be put off by such a reply because he may find himself dealing with someone who is quite shy or, perhaps, not prepared to venture an opinion. Others will be more forthcoming and present him with a list of ailments, imaginary or otherwise. With all of these people, the coach needs to establish the rapport best suited to the individual bowler with whom he is working, and show himself to be a good listener. The qualities of patience and tolerance are very important factors in conducting a successful clinic session.

People of all ages attend these clinics because they wish to improve their game. There is also always a wide range of shapes and figures, both male and female, and here the coach must be exceptionally careful, for it would not do to offend anyone with a hasty or flippant remark. Neither would it be acceptable to pre-judge any person simply from appearance. Fashion and personal adornment have changed considerably over the last few years but, no matter how they appear, the coach must reserve judgement and not jump to a hasty, and sometimes mistaken, first impression.

The language used by the coach is extremely important during such clinic sessions. He should remember that the bowler is not fully at ease. The coach need not state the obvious, for example, saying to a person who bumps the bowl on delivery, 'You are bumping the bowl'; the player knows that only too well. It would be kinder to say, 'I think there was a slight bump there – do you agree?' and then suggest that they work together to see if they can get rid of it. The invitation to 'work together' is one that rarely fails to set the bowler more at ease. The coach is identifying with the bowler and his problem, and not setting himself apart.

Language is the main method of communication and it would be well if the coach approached the bowler with quiet questions and suggestions rather than dogma. 'Can you just try it this way?' is probably better than 'Do it this way'. Persuasion will usually bring about the best response from the player. The timely and wise use of humour is another important asset the coach can use and again this helps to relax the player.

Of course, the range of bowlers who may seek advice from a coach can be very wide, varying from those who depend entirely upon the coach to those who may be waiting for the coach to make the slightest error. Coaches should be aware of, and prepared to deal with, both types of people because they can both drain a coach physically and emotionally, and if this is allowed to happen, the clinic session could be a disaster.

The coach, if he is to work successfully, has to be so many things to so many people. It may sound like stating the obvious to point out that coaches need not be rigid in their approach. They must be flexible and adaptable and never risk losing the confidence of the person who has plucked up enough courage to ask for help. Often, when working with bowlers at such clinics, the coach may become aware of a number of people gathered around because they are interested in watching and listening to what is going on. Their presence could place both coach and player under additional pressure. The coach must deal with this, remembering always that his priority is with the bowler.

It can happen that a coach is approached by a player at the end of an evening game, complaining about some shortcoming in his play. Perhaps the coach may decide there and then to offer immediate assistance. However, if a clinic session has been planned in advance, it is important that the coach is correctly dressed for the occasion. Correct dress should be as laid down in club rules and, of course, a better impression will be made by being smartly turned out.

Video Coaching Clinics

The English Bowls Coaching Scheme is fortunate to have the expertise of Kelvin Carr, who has designed a split-screen facility for use in coaching clinics. There are, of course, many thousands of bowlers of several years' experience, who have never seen themselves in action, and many are attracted to the video clinics for this aspect alone. However, the majority who attend do so because their game has deteriorated for one reason or another.

The video is an excellent visual aid when used correctly by the coach who, having asked the bowler to deliver a bowl on the forehand and then on the backhand, will invite him to come and see himself on the television screen. Because of the split-screen facility, the bowler can see a front and back view of his delivery action.

Many bowlers are surprised to see how they deliver the bowl, and will sometimes comment that they were unaware that they did such-and-such a thing. One young lady bowler, for example, was astonished to see from the television screen that, at the moment of delivery, her non-bowling arm had been flung back and in fact was above her head. The result was that on almost every delivery her bowling hand had to be placed on the green to prevent her from falling forward. Once having seen it on the screen for herself, she was anxious to correct it, since she confessed that until then she had had no idea why she lost balance at the completion of the delivery action.

The Coach should discuss with the bowler any faults in his play that he has witnessed and then set about remedial practice to rectify them.

The demands placed upon coaches from all areas and directions can be quite considerable. He may leave the green thoroughly drained but often the rewards outweigh all other considerations. Helping people overcome minor or major difficulties, seeing frowns replaced by smiles, and knowing that the bowler will now be able to enjoy his next game all the more, is as much as anyone can ask.

11 The 5 Cs of Flat Green Bowling

Every year, many thousands of men and women battle through round after round of county competitions in order to qualify for their national championships. The English Women's Bowling Association hold theirs at Leamington, and the English Bowling Association finals are held at Worthing. Obviously, motivation is there to make them play, in the early part of the season, on some indifferent greens and in inclement weather, and even when they reach the Leamington or Worthing venues, there are still several games to play in singles, pairs, triples and fours before they reach the finals stage. But imagine the prize – Singles Champion of England, or Singles Champion of the British Isles!

Most bowlers, when asked what they believe are the qualities necessary to become a winner would quote the '5 Cs':

concentration
consistency
confidence
competitiveness
compatibility

There could be others that bowlers might add and their lists may differ in order of what they consider to be the priority area. Perhaps confidence and consistency could arise quite easily in players who have an abundance of natural talent, but it has often been said that bowls is 'a funny old game' and this has been borne out by many results that completely confounded the pun-

dits. So what is it all about? We are talking about a game which demands that the player demonstrates the ability to deliver a bowl which travels in a curved line to a spot on the green some 30yd (27.4m) away. It sounds quite simple but, to be successful, players will have to employ some or all of the 'Cs'.

CONCENTRATION

Concentration is a word that has been bandied about by coaches in most sports, and crops up frequently in end of term reports, where its lack is often cited as one of the causes for a less than satisfactory outcome. It is important to remember that applying concentration during a practice session is just as necesary as applying it during a game. It is natural that we are able to concentrate and strengthen those areas of a game that we can already do well, because all sportspersons enjoy succeeding, but the bowler who wishes to be really successful must apply far more concentration to those areas of indifferent perfomance. All players need a degree of honesty in admitting that certain areas need to be worked at, so that whatever situation arises in a game, they will have the confidence to tackle it.

The following is a check-list of some of the factors that can damage concentration, in an actual game situation, which you should be aware of:

1.   Negative thinking, e.g. fear of failure.
2.   Noise level, especially at indoor greens.
3.   Incorrect mental preparation.
4.   Trying too hard to concentrate.
5.   The behaviour of opponent(s).
6.   Partisanship of the spectators working against you.
7.   Recalling a previous occasion when you played a similar shot with a poor result.
8.   The fact that you, or your team, are well behind on the score-card.
9.   Any doubts about the playing surface.
10.   Inclement weather conditions, such as rain or strong wind.
11.   Adverse circumstances, causing you to arrive at the green just as the game is due to start.
12.   Any sort of disagreement during the game.
13.   The fact that someone you wish to impress is watching the game.
14.   Being not entirely in agreement with the views of your skip regarding selection of shot.

All of these can have a detrimental effect in differing degrees on individual players. Of course, the list is not complete because there are those who have their personal catalogue of factors that can affect concentration. But, as with confidence, it is important that players recognize that there are certain things that can affect their powers of concentration. The trick is to be prepared and have some system of protection that can be employed to diminish their effects on your game.

Bowls is a game that can demand the inch-perfect playing of a shot over 30yd (27.4m) or more. This cannot be achieved without concentration, but what is really meant by this word? Everyone agrees it is necessary in any game of skill but it can mean so many different things to so many people. Some bowlers will pick up the bowl, adopt their stance on the mat, and will have delivered the bowl in a matter of a few seconds. When did they apply concentration? Even before picking up the bowl, were they able to visualize the line the bowl would need to take and mentally compute the speed at which they needed to deliver the bowl? Others will take a longer time on the mat and appear to apply concentration for several seconds before actually releasing the bowl. Others adopt a ritual of preparation prior to releasing the bowl. This ritual has a comforting effect upon the bowler and is a repetition of something he has done many hundreds of times. Stance, grip, back-swing and all other elements of the delivery action are completely grooved-in, so they require no conscious effort. He does it from memory and can therefore clear his mind and employ complete concentration.

How concentration is applied, depends upon the player as a person, rather than purely as a bowler. There are those who can switch on their powers of concentration whenever it is needed. Others prefer to try to concentrate on each bowl, including those bowled by an opponent. Perhaps this is over-stretching the capability for constant concentration. Once a bowl has left the hand of any opponent, no amount of concentration is likely to alter the result. However, the result may alter radically the next shot you have to play, and it is your next shot that is so important, and demands your total concentration.

Some might argue that, because of the nature of the game, bowls does not require this extreme behaviour, but it depends on the degree of success or standard that any bowler may wish to achieve. Since all play-

Fig 94   Carl Lewis intent on getting the right line.

ers have every intention of bowling the perfect bowl each time, even if they do feel that they are only playing 'for fun', then surely whatever means they employ to encourage the necessary concentration must be important. Therefore, perhaps we can look at some of the factors that could be an aid to concentration:

1. The ability to be calm and unruffled, while still being eager to play.
2. Receiving generous support from other players in the team.
3. Having read the green well from the outset.
4. Having had the time to prepare thoroughly for the game.
5. Playing against people whose company you enjoy.
6. Putting behind you any indifferent shot, or shots, you may have played, and devoting all your attention to the next bowl you are to play.
7. Being able to conjure up at will, any mental image that supports or maintains your concentration.

Relaxation

The word 'concentration' can conjure up several mental images: the young child, forming letters for the first time, with pencil poised over paper, tongue protruding, and exuding an air of intensity; or the furrowed brow and frowning face of a person taking their first driving lesson. However, it is not always correct to associate concentration with worry or fear of failure, and indeed having these two very negative feelings could contribute to impairing concentration. It could be that the bowler who, when concentrating, has a relaxed look about him, may be more successful than the bowler who wears a frown. The frown may indicate that other matters and other thoughts are cluttering the mind, thus reducing the degree of concentration.

Nowadays there are well established and documented techniques to aid relaxation and mental preparation. Information on such matters is available from organizations such as the National Coaching Foundation. The guidance and suggestions they offer can be used by bowlers, and are not exclusive to certain sports.

To have to face a situation where you have several shots against you could be described as stressful, especially if you have just one bowl left to play. If the bowler feels that he is under stress, it might be a good idea not to rush into playing that final bowl. He could slow down all activity and breathe more deeply and more slowly, as this can be conducive to clearing the mind so that total concentration can be brought to bear on the bowl to be delivered. A conscious application of slowing down everything is also an exercise in improving self-control, and a player must be fully in control before he even thinks about bowling the next bowl. Any anxiety that is experienced can result in an overall feeling of tension throughout the body. This will certainly affect the bowling arm, and hence the delivery of the bowl. Do not wait until you are faced with such a situation on the green. Quite simple relaxation can be practised at home.

How you bring yourself to the necessary pitch for concentrating on whatever bowling challenge you may be facing will probably be personal to yourself, but you must be able to depend upon it and use it constantly if you are to play to the maximum of your potential. Remember that those things that harm your concentration come from without but true concentration comes from within. There is no off-pat answer to the problem of losing concentration, except to say that the bowler must exercise this inner discipline and develop sufficient strength of character to overcome the problem.

CONSISTENCY

This is probably the most elusive element in the game of bowls and possibly in all major sports. Most bowlers have experienced the frustration of having an excellent game on Monday and a poor game on Tuesday. Perhaps a great deal of soul searching goes on after such an experience in trying to analyse or rationalize exactly what went wrong. It would be too simplistic to say, 'It was just not my day', because there must be reasons and relevant factors that were important for both the good and the poor game.

It is probable that the stars of the game make fewer mistakes than most because they have developed their skills to such a degree that confidence and concentration flow quite easily into consistency, with each being an integral part of the whole. But how is this achieved? Obviously such players do have a great deal of natural ability and talent to offer, and there is no real substitute for such gifts, but that is not to say that the skills necessary to play the game to a high standard cannot be improved with sound and purposeful practice.

It would seem to be not too difficult to get both line and length correct, time after time, and so it would be if all bowlers were radio-controlled robots. Happily, this is not the case: human error and misjudgements will play an important part in any overall result, but these can be minimized.

We can begin with correct reading of the green. Probably, no two bowling greens will

offer exactly the same sort of playing surface, and so the bowler must decide firstly whether it is a fast, slow or heavy green; and he must look for any irregularities on the playing surface that will affect the speed of the bowl or the line the bowl takes, for example, a section along the green that keeps the bowl running in a more or less straight line for longer than normal. These are just a few of the vagaries that bowlers will have to be prepared for before they can consistently bowl that correct line and length.

Even when the green, or playing surface, has been read correctly, bowlers then have to actually propel the bowl so that it achieves the objective. The bowler must have absolute faith in the delivery action he is employing – one small error in delivery can be magnified several times by the time the bowl has come to rest. It is important to emphasize that the whole body is involved in the delivery action. Therefore, all movement must be controlled, correct and conducive to bowling a bowl which will gain the best possible result.

During a game, bowlers do not always bowl directly at the jack. They may be required to play a shot beyond or to the right or left of where the jack is positioned. This will mean that the bowler will have to find a new line and length, and there is always the possibility that this new line travels over a section of the rink that has not been played on very much at all, with the probability that the bowl will slow down slightly. Such factors must be borne in mind when the weight with which we need to bowl is being 'computed' and then decided. Indeed, bowls is a game that demands minor adjustments to be made continually by the bowler. The most difficult way to do this is to leave it until it arises during any game situation. At most bowling clubs, members will have ex-

Fig 95 Stephen Rees.

perienced changes in the playing surface, even during the course of a few days. Rarely does any green behave in exactly the same way time after time. Therefore, to improve consistency, the bowler will need to practise and practise as often as possible. This should be well planned so that with almost every bowl the player is having to make some adjustments in length and line. The reward for this diligence should be an increased enjoyment of the game.

CONFIDENCE

Confidence-building is an essential area of pre-match preparation, if you are to play to your best ability. Once the game begins, your confidence must never be lost. If you are inadvertently given the wrong information by the marker or you miss, by a fraction, some shots you played, or your opponent destroys some good bowling by you with the use of heavy bowls, it is easy for your confidence to waver. Therefore, it is essential to adopt a strategy for regaining faith in your ability.

One very famous bowler lost a count of four on one end, in a singles game, but then gained a count of four on the next end. His rationalization was that, although he had dropped four shots, he himself had bowled four good bowls. This was the priority for his pattern of thinking for the follow-

Fig 96   So smoothly away.

ing end, and resulted in him retrieving the four shots he had lost on the previous end. This serves as an excellent demonstration of strength of character and belief in oneself. His opponent, meanwhile, having gained a maximum count, allowed his concentration to slip a little.

Self-confidence is also necessary when playing in a pairs, triples of fours game. Here the ethos can be different from the game of singles. If one player in the pairs, triples or fours game is playing exceptionally well, this can provide a springboard for boosting the confidence of the other players and this will be manifested in their speech and their entire body-language. They may have an air of invincibility and attempt difficult and sometimes dangerous shots with a seemingly cavalier approach – and almost always execute them perfectly.

As one side's confidence increases, that of the opposing side usually decreases (unless, of course, they each recognize what is happening and consciously repair their own approach to the game and mend the damage done to their confidence). The obverse of this is that as one side's confidence decreases, the opposing team's ego is given a boost. Therefore, when any combination of players begin to feel confidence ebbing away, the last thing for them to do is to demonstrate, or reveal, this to their opponents. A team should not, of course, rely on the flagging spirits of the other team to keep them high, but must actively promote their own sense of well-being from within.

Confidence should not be confused with conceit or arrogance, as this can carry the seed of downfall. If arrogance is once dented, the graph line of loss of confidence will travel downward at a much faster rate. Confidence should rather be allied to a disciplined conviction that you will continue to bowl to the best of your ability in spite of any circumstances that could occur during a game.

COMPETITIVENESS

Possibly one of the best-known expressions in sport is 'the will to win', and competitiveness is a necessary quality for any player in any game. When bowlers engage in competition, they will first wish to demonstrate their bowling skills in the hope that whatever they have to offer may prove good enough to beat their opponent. However, they should also demonstrate a good standard of etiquette, sportsmanship and a respect for the laws of the game and they should endeavour to play the game in such a way that they gain the respect of their opponent. This last will be more to do with them as people, rather than as players.

Comments such as 'He is a good competitor' or 'He is a difficult bowler to beat' are often as much comments about that particular player as a person as they are about his skill as a bowler. So what characteristics does a good competitor demonstrate? The key words are probably 'ability' and 'performance'. He will have prepared himself as thoroughly as possible by analysing any faults in his playing performance and working to eliminate them. Therefore, he will have the ability and confidence to attempt any shot and will demonstrate such an aura of self-belief that he is likely to overawe the opponent. The personality of his fellow competitor will have been gauged carefully, to ensure that nothing is done or said that will boost his confidence. At all times, such a bowler will be perfectly in control of himself and his game, even under intense pressure. By retaining total concentration throughout, he will know

Fig 97   Note the concentration on David Bryant's Face.

exactly what is required, perhaps controlled aggression in the playing of one shot, and yet the next minute a feather-touch bowl ending in the perfect draw. Never will he allow his opponent to dominate him or put him off by any use of gamesmanship, but will fight all the way.

Even this paragon of a player will sometimes lose a game of bowls but, with the preparations and qualities listed above, he will be able to rise above that failure and repair his competitive spirit for the next game. This will be possible because he is totally committed to playing competitive bowls at a high standard. It should be pointed out here that a loser may have none the less contributed greatly to a match that spectators and players alike have enjoyed immensely, and so has every right to come out of it with head held high.

The vast majority of bowlers who enter competitions at national, county or club level will possibly never have thought along the lines that were adopted by our fictional bowler. So many people will find themselves hurrying home from a working day, eating a quick meal, then dashing off to the bowling venue – not much time for programmed preparation here. However, they can still give a good account of themselves against the opposition, and play to the best of their abilities by taking with them a determination to make their way through to the next round. Perhaps they will display a touch of daring here, or caution there, and even full-blooded aggression under certain circumstances, a smile, a clap, a wry expression, depending on the ebb and flow of the game.

Most bowlers who go on to higher levels of competition will probably have developed a taste for such competitive bowling by first winning the club singles, pairs, triples or fours. Probably, there are many hundreds of bowlers who enter these kinds of tournaments or competitions simply to 'have a go'. They may not expect to get very far but they relish the opportunity to play at a competitive level that does not come their way all that often. The experience should help them to become more complete and competitively minded players, and having that spirit within them is one of the necessary ingredients required to produce a player of real standing.

COMPATIBILITY

This is another of those words cited so frequently by bowlers as being an attribute to be cultivated and developed by players. The very nature of the game allows players the time to be together, both at the mat and at the head. At both places, and without infringing on the etiquette necessary in the game, they can converse and such conversations will probably be to do with the progress of the game, or the last bowl played, or indeed any talking point that arises quite naturally from the play. This can be part of a 'getting to know you' exercise, especially when players have never met before with their team mates. In a game that can throw peopel together for a period of some three hours, knowing and understanding the other players is a necessary ingredient of what can be described as 'rink harmony'.

It is in the interest of all four members of a rink that they play well together and for each other. But this does not just involve getting to know your playing partners because rink harmony goes much deeper than that. Many will say that it would be up to the skip to create a good spirit within the rink. To a degree, there is some truth in this statement but, in the same way that each of the four bowlers will be expected to make a contribution by their play, it is equally true that other forms of contribution are necessary to promote good rink spirit, and that all four have important parts to play in achieving this.

It could be a mistake to suggest that compatibility within a rink can always be achieved by having one dominant and three subservient players, since most people are different in attitudes, behaviour patterns, strengths and weaknesses, and therefore there can be no hard and fast rules. Indeed, the bringing together of four quite different personalities and welding them into a cohesive four is quite a gamble. Of course the skip does have the responsibility of creating an ethos to which the other three can respond and give of their best, but each player must recognize, very quickly, the correct form of contribution that he can personally offer. It is obvious that they have to be supportive of each other throughout the game but what form should that support take?

Some players respond to a noisy and overt form of congratulation on having played a good bowl. Others could be slightly embarrassed by this. Equally there seems little point in being over-conciliatory at the playing of a poor bowl. The saying 'least said, soonest mended' often applies in this situation. There can also be the case of team mates attempting to 'lift' a player who is not having a very good game by congratulating him after he has played a mediocre bowl. The player in question knows that he has not played the shot well and could suffer acute embarrassment by such a reaction from the rest of his rink. This will do nothing to bolster his confidence, but simply fuel his feeling of being the 'poor relation'. The response of the other players may have been given with the best

of intentions, but they had not read the attitude of their playing partner very well at all, and this is very important because if his confidence is severely dented, this will affect the next bowl he has to play.

To watch a rink that has played together for some time is an education in itself. Compatibility has been built up over a period of time and is now well established. The players will ooze self-confidence and belief in the team as a formidable four. That is not to say that each will have the same psychological profile, or indeed the same skills to offer, but it is evident that they have arrived at a degree of compatibility that suits the rink as a whole. They will probably have exercised a personal discipline for the good of the rink. They adopt their individual roles each time they play together and, even though they may not be the best bowlers, as a team they may well prove to be a difficult combination to overcome. They will demonstrate that ability always to attempt what will prove best for the rink, although this does not suggest that there will be no difference of opinion. Within a rink of such compatibility, there will still be intense discussion about the shot to be played but, once a decision has been made, they will then offer whole-hearted support to the player who has to play the shot. Collective decisions will usually be more common from such a rink than individual decisions and it is this total involvement that is but one result of the degree of compatibility they have achieved.

It is in adversity that the strength of a rink will be best demonstrated. Human error has to be accepted as a part of any game and if this should happen there will, of course, be disappointment, but no frowns or scowls of reproval. Only one player can play a shot at any given time but the rink should be totally involved during the time

Fig 98   Wynne Richards sums up the situation.

the shot is being played. From the moment the bowl leaves the hand of their player, they will offer it encouragement and, by so doing, will also be reinforcing their complete faith in the bowler. If the bowl does not achieve what they hoped, their support of the player should, of course, continue.

This degree of compatibility is a precious asset to any rink of four players, as it would be in a pairs or triples game. It does not happen by accident, nor is it God given, but must be worked at just as hard as the playing side of the game.

There are occasions when opponents can actually assist the compatibility of a rink. If there is a player among the opposing four who has a slightly belligerent attitude, is loud with his opinions, and clearly shows displeasure towards any of his own rink who may not have played a very good shot, he is proving that he has no idea of what compatibility is. Undoubtedly, he is playing into the hands of his opponents by providing an excellent demonstration of how not to behave. He is a disruptive element in the harmony of his own rink, and a positive element in helping to build comradeship in the opposing rink. Such players are probably playing purely for themselves; they want to win, of course, but are quite unable to see or recognize the real importance of the colleagues playing with them or indeed to understand that their own contribution is actually proving to be counter-productive.

Any discussion on rink harmony cannot be left without further mention of the very important role of the skip. His temperament, behaviour, encouragement and demonstration of bowling skill will be paramount in guiding his rink towards compatibility. He must not quash natural exuberance and will need to help lift anyone of an introverted character. He must clearly show the charisma necessary for leadership. His comments will need to be made after careful thought but appear to be genuinely spontaneous. he must clearly show a depth of knowledge about the strategies and tactics of the game in order that he gains the trust of his players. He must read each player so that he will know exactly the ploy to use to get them to give their best. He must judge the precise time to confer, to listen, and when to make his own views known in such a way that does not offend any other members of his rink. He must attempt to be all things to all his players as it is from the platform he provides that true compatibility can grow. When this begins to happen, he must nourish it most carefully. His responsibilities to his players are legion and, as his own conduct will be constantly under the microscope, his own bowling performance should be such that he leads by example.

Compatibility is a very important aspect of successful rink play and each player shares the responsibility of promoting it, each in his own way and to his own measure. No player can afford to stand outside, aloof and alone; this can only be detrimental to the rink as a whole. Each player must strive hard for the good of the whole and, before long, he will feel proud to belong in a rink which has achieved that important quality.

12 The Short Mat Game

The short mat game began in Ireland and was later introduced into this country. There now exists the English Short Mat Bowling Association, which is supported by regional associations. The game has its own set of rules, and any prospective player would do well to be conversant with them before playing the game proper.

As the title implies, the game is played over a much shorter length than the flat green game. The carpet is between 40–45ft (12.2–13.7m) and 6ft (1.8m) wide. At both ends, there is a fender, and 1ft (0.3m) in from the fender there is a white line, representing the ditch. There are other white markings on the carpet but players would be best appraised of the reasons for such markings by studying the rule book.

Equipment to be used is the same as that for playing on the larger indoor or outdoor surfaces. There are regulations as regards the weight or size of the bowl to be used but, in the main, those who have the necessary equipment for playing the outdoor or full-length indoor flat green game would be correctly set up to play the short mat game.

The basic skills required for playing the short mat game are exactly those for playing the flat green game outdoors and indoors. These are, of course, line and length. Any short mat player must practise and perfect both as far as it is possible. He must develop a good 'eye' for the line and a good 'feel' for the weight he needs to bowl a correct length. The fact that normal-size bowls can be used will also assist the player in developing his individual grip. He will also learn that it is essential to get the body as close to the playing surface as possible, and he will certainly learn the importance of the speed of the arm coming through to enable him to bowl the required length.

Because the mat is only 40–45ft (12.2–13.7m) long, it can be laid on a large variety of surfaces, providing the surface is flat, and so leisure centres can be used. Usually more than one carpet can be laid because such centres offer an abundance of floor space. Halls of every description are usually acceptable, even if the carpet has to be laid diagonally. Short mat offers the extra bonus that the carpet can be taken up, rolled and stored away at the completion of the games, thereby enabling the hall to be used for any other function.

It is yet another advantage of the game that players can be protected from the weather and are therefore reasonably sure that they can play their game at the date and time arranged. There are several bowling clubs who play the short mat game during the winter months in their club pavilions and it has been known for some to extend their existing pavilions to accommodate this short mat. Such actions speak volumes for the popularity of the game as a whole.

As well as the reduced length, the short mat game has also introduced a block. This block is 15in (4.6cm) long, 3in (7.6cm) high and not more than 3in wide, and is placed at the centre and across the mat. Any bowl that touches the block on its course along the carpet is declared 'dead' and removed. It also has another purpose. Over such a

The Short Mat Game

short distance, it would not be too difficult for a bowler to use a heavy bowl to disturb or break up the head. The block can effectively prevent this from happening and, therefore, the majority of shots that will be played will be drawing shots. Of course, if a jack has been moved off the centre line, a player of some skill could still use the heavier bowl to gain an advantage but the use of the block has certainly influenced players to think of the drawing shot as being the most important shot to learn, which is a positive point as it is basic to the playing of the game, no matter what length of carpet or rink is used.

The growth of the short mat game has been quite startling in so short a period of time. The example of one county, that went from nine short mat clubs to more than eighty over a two-year period speaks for itself. This kind of growth has been particularly evident in areas such as the South West, but it would be wrong to think that it is confined to predominantly rural areas. There has always been the grumble that there is not much to do in such rural areas during the winter months, but it would be an over-simplification to suggest that this is the main reason for the popularity of this game. Indeed, there is evidence that the short mat game has an enormous attraction for many thousands of bowlers in all parts of the country.

It would also be somewhat naive to imagine that short mat clubs are mere 'nurseries' for the outdoor or indoor flat green game. However, it must be said that many people do turn to the short mat game because they are unable to join a flat green bowling club that is already over-subscribed, and probably has a waiting list. The short mat might also give some players the appetite to play on larger surfaces and, if they live in parts of the country where they are able to join bowling clubs, they can fulfil that appetite.

One group of bowlers who benefit greatly from the short mat game is the disabled. There is obviously no great physical input required, and for those in wheelchairs there is an ease of movement from the mat to the opposite end of the playing area that they would not find in either an indoor or an outdoor bowling green.

The players of short mat bowls are no less competitive than their counterparts who play on the larger playing surfaces, and this is quite evident from the league structures that now exist. Results and league placings are published in local newspapers and are avidly scanned by those who wish to work out the possible chances for promotion or indeed demotion. Also, since 1986, International Series between England, Scotland, Ireland and Wales have been staged, as well as championship matches. It would be equally wrong to assume that the short mat game is any less exciting. Bowlers demonstrate the same keenness, dedication, skill and determination as they do in the outdoor game. There is no less delight at having played a good bowl, as the length of the carpet does not affect the obvious pleasure of succeeding in beating your opponent.

The age range of those wishing to participate in the short mat game is even wider than that of the outdoor game. Young people of even eight or nine years of age take part, and the youngest, in my personal experience, was just six years of age. These could prove to be good 'seed-corn' for the future of the game as a whole. Admittedly, some younger players may find it difficult to hold even the smallest bowl allowed by the rules but they are still learning so many other important things, especially the etiquette of the game.

There seems to be no reason why interest and participation in the short mat game should not continue to flourish. There will be a number of players who may never wish to play on any larger surface, but always stay with the short mat game of bowls. As in all sports, the majority of people like to win, but possibly more important still is the enjoyment that any game has to offer. This enjoyment appears to be abundantly evident in so far as the short mat game is concerned and, therefore, it will retain its devotees and practitioners and its status as a game in its own right.

13 Bowling for All Abilities

YOUNG PEOPLE AND BOWLS

The English Bowls Coaching Scheme has, for several years, carried out coaching with young players, both male and female, ranging from ten to eighteen years of age, and the standard of skill demonstrated by these young players has been most en-couraging. Many followed parental prefer-ence for the game but there were others who came into bowls entirely of their own accord. It is interesting to find that a lot of the present-day stars of the bowling world began at a very young age (although that is not to say they eschewed other sports). This early beginning must have had a posi-tive effect on shaping their future prowess.

Fig 99   The author coaching young women bowls players.

What schools can offer young people today has certainly widened, when compared with several years ago, in terms of physical education and games. Many schools, during summer terms, offer an activity week where young people can choose a particular activity and there are now several who choose to be taught the game of bowls. At this time of year, there are several indoor bowling clubs which can offer their facilities for such groups. Of course, it will be an advantage if there is a member of staff who has had some experience of the game itself but, failing that, the guide-lines offered in Chapter 2, which provide some ideas on how to introduce a beginner to the game of bowls, can be followed. The ideal situation would be that a member of staff has already qualified as an instructor for beginners under the English Bowls Coaching Scheme. However, many indoor clubs have at least one qualified coach and usually they are prepared to give their time in helping to introduce young people to the game.

These early sessions are very important. The instructor must use his skills in establishing the correct rapport with the group, so as to foster and encourage their initial interest. This calls for great skill on the part of the instructor as a communicator, and is vital for the overall success of the session(s). He must ensure that a range of sets of bowls are available for the group, as well as correct footwear. Some coaches allow beginners to play in stocking feet but this is not always a good idea. Practical preparation is important before such a session so that all necessary equipment is at hand because, like all of us, young people do not enjoy having to wait about.

Rather than dealing with just one bowler at a time, and have others sitting around, it would be sensible to involve them all. If there is a group of six, the other five could be invited to step on to the green so that they could listen to and watch what was taking place. After the first bowler had gone through the exercise of delivering the jack to the coach's satisfaction then the others could, in turn, be asked to do the same. The whole group needs to be involved in the learning process so that everybody's interest is maintained.

Following the jack rolling, each member of the group could then be asked to pick up a bowl. Not everyone will choose the bowl best suited to them but the coach should allow free discussion and for them to make mistakes. It can be very easy with such a group for the coach to impose his ideas but this must not happen as each player needs to be encouraged to think for himself as an individual, and express his own opinions.

There is one group of schools in the Bristol area that do not have to rely on the availability of indoor greens, as they have been fortunate enough to find sponsorship which provides them with short mats (45ft/13.7m long). This is the way many young people have been introduced to the game of bowls and it does create an appetite for playing on a full-size green. Generally, young people can be quick to adapt to the demands of a full-size green, making use of the skills they have already learned.

Younger bowlers are now finding a welcome at club level. They can represent the 'seed-corn' for the future, not only for a club, but for the game. International matches and inter-county matches for teams of under 25s are now well established for both men and women. Full international squads now have a much younger average age than they had some years ago. Therefore, a great deal of encouragement can be found for any young person who wishes to take up the game of bowls.

Such encouragement offered by more experienced players or club officials can only be good for the future of the game. The suppleness and athleticism of young players and the ease of their smooth delivery action may be the envy of more elderly members, but the game only begins with the delivery action – there is much more to learn. I have been pleasantly surprised by the receptiveness of young players to coaching. The eagerness to listen, to learn and to improve their game is very evident. The game cannot afford to lose this enthusiasm and thirst for improvement, but must channel it into well-planned coaching sessions, which include discussions on such issues as how a shot is selected, and practices that are purposeful and have been carefully explained by the coach, so that the young players have a clear understanding of the achievement level expected of them.

Under the guidance of the coach, the game can be 'frozen' to allow general discussion about, for example, the options open to the next person to bowl. Are there any percentage or conversion shots available? What possibility is there of something going very wrong? Throughout such exercises, the coach must always frame his speech in the form of questions and never demand that a bowler play this or that shot. He must encourage discussion, prompt argument, and be sure that all players are invited to make their point of view known to the group. He must know the exact moment to stop the talking and invite the player to play the shot he has opted for.

As soon as the bowl has come to rest, the head, in all probability, has changed again, so discussion begins on the next shot to be played. This activity has been labelled 'freezing the head' and has been enthusiastically received. young bowlers, in particular, relish the opportunities for voicing their own opinions, as well as recognizing that they are improving their knowledge of the game generally. They also bring to this exercise a youthful exuberance that the good coach will use wisely, in order to motivate sound positive thinking and build confidence.

There are several other areas of the game where such exercises can be used to further overall knowledge of playing the game of bowls, but it is important to stress that such practices should take place on the green and should always be related to the actual game situation. Coaches should always plan such practices very carefully, and any bowls he uses in preparing for them should be placed judiciously. The players should be made aware of the score, and the end being played, and a situation should never be created where one bowl could bring about an abrupt end to the session, i.e. by tracking the jack into the ditch.

Encouragement must be offered to young bowlers on every possible occasion. The game of bowls will benefit from their participation and it should follow that standards of performance will steadily improve.

BOWLS PLAYERS WITH DISABILITIES

The word 'disability' covers a very wide spectrum, including the blind, the partially sighted, wheelchair bowlers and those with a mental handicap. Some instructors of the English Bowls Coaching Scheme devote many hours of their time to helping the above groups to enjoy their game of bowls. There are also bowlers with no coaching qualifications who perform admirable work with disabled bowlers.

Since the game of bowls demands a limited physical input, it is not surprising that many people who are disabled in one form or another can achieve some measure of success in the game. There is now a chair available for wheelchair bowlers, which has been especially designed to leave no mark or imprint on the playing surface. This is called the Bradshaw Buggy and can be custom built for the particular needs of the individual bowler. Many bowling clubs have purchased such a chair and make it available for any person in a wheelchair who wishes to use it.

To assist the blind and partially sighted, a string can be placed along the centre line of the rink. By touching the string the bowler can help to orientate himself on the mat, to line up the body with the line they wish to adopt to play a particular shot. The coach at the head can feed back information to the bowler by using the clock method, so that if a bowl delivered on a correct line comes to rest some 4ft (1.2m) beyond the jack, he will be informed that the bowl has come to rest at 12 o'clock and is 4ft (1.2m) beyond the jack. If the bowl had been delivered on the correct line, but comes to rest 4ft (1.2m) short, its position would be given as 6 o'clock and 4ft (1.2m) short. This

Fig 100 Paul Hubbal in the Bradshaw Buggy, playing a demonstration match with Brian Kingdom.

Fig 101   Bowls players using the Bradshaw Buggy, with its designer,
Peter Bradshaw.

constant flow of information is very important but equally important is the way in which it is given, bearing in mind that the keynote should always be one of encouragement.

Mentally handicapped bowlers, especially those with Down's Syndrome, seem to enjoy the game very much indeed. When encouraged and persuaded to play, statistics seem to support the fact that it has a beneficial effect upon their behaviour patterns. It is sometimes difficult for them to communicate their feelings to those who work with them but to watch their faces when they have bowled a good bowl is a tremendous reward in itself.

Gratitude must be expressed to all those bowling clubs, both outdoor and indoor, who place their facilities at the disposal of coaches and players with disabilities.

BOWLS PLAYERS OF ADVANCING YEARS

Bowls can be played to a grand old age. But old age is usually accompanied by some stiffening of joints. Some simple exercises have already been suggested in the section on Physical Preparation in Chapter 7, which could help to keep the joints supple.

By and large, it would seem that knee joints are often more affected than others and this could mean that a complete re-appraisal of the delivery action is needed. It is surprising how often a bowler can help himself by simply bending the knees before the forward stride is attempted. This bending action helps to lower the body nearer to the playing surface and can help to ensure that the bowl is not bumped on delivery. Some older bowlers find this slight change awkward or uncomfortable, but this is, in the main, a question of adjustment after many years of bowling from a particular stance. Of course it will feel strange but perseverence is necessary.

Some bowlers of an advanced age may feel it necessary to take a long forward stride so that the bowl will travel the required distance along the green. This can mean a bowl being pitched out of the hand instead of being rolled smoothly off the fingers, and can also result in loss of balance, causing the bowler to end his delivery action with one hand on the green to prevent himself falling forward. Therefore, the length of stride is important and bowlers need to think more about the speed of the arm coming through to deliver the bowl, rather than trying to compensate with a too long forward stride.

Wrists and fingers can often become less supple, especially if there is a touch of arthritis. Now could be the time for the bowler to think carefully about the grip that he uses. Some slight alteration may be necessary, especially in the position of the thumb, so that the bowl can be held comfortably and without undue strain. In some cases, it could be that a smaller set of

bowls might help but it would be advisable to consult a bowls coach before making any undue expenditure. Many bowlers in the more elderly category have been helped by good bowls coaches, and encouraged to make some adjustments that will allow a smoother delivery action without unnecesssary strain.

Some of the more elderly bowlers tend to make their own re-adjustments. The danger here lies in the fact that there now could occur a multiplicity of changes which can aggravate the original problem, resulting in a less than enjoyable experience when playing a game. It could be better to consult a good coach, since the 'eye' of the coach could identify a difficulty or difficulties at a very early stage and could then offer sound advice that may provide a remedy for the problem. It needs to be said that when the coach has offered good advice, the onus then falls squarely on the bowler to carry it out and to work hard, even with minor changes, to accustom himself to these differences. It will not be easy and will demand total concentration and determination.

Some bowlers of more advanced years may realize that their performance in the game is not as good as it used to be. No coach can do anything to remedy increasing age, and it could be more to the point if the bowler himself accepted the truth of the situation. This is not meant to be harsh but realistic, as it would be better if the bowler suited his ambiitions in the game to his present performance. Some bowlers, perhaps, do not like the idea of having to surrender a skip position because their game is not what it was, but there are other positions in the rink which they can play and where they can continue to make a positive contribution. Certainly their experience in the tactics of the game would be valuable and they could find themselves guiding along a younger club member, thereby creating for themselves an even more enjoyable experience.

THE GAME OF BOWLS – THE END RESULT

Like most games, bowls offers the opportunity for players to perform to the best of their potential, and provides a source of great enjoyment for each player. It appears to be a game that can be played in a calm and quiet way, where there does not seem to be too great a physical demand made upon any participant. It seems to be measured and methodical, deliberate and disciplined, as befits a game of great skill. But this description can be misleading because, in the heat of competitive play, players will demonstrate a wide range of emotions. The game can provide moments of great joy or deep disappointment, euphoria or despair.

Bowls demands concentration and control, courage and caution, decisiveness and a delicacy of touch. It requests true sportsmanship and an honest appreciation of an opponent's skill, without losing belief in oneself and the determination to win. It needs strict mental application with a tight control over any negative thoughts, and the physical and emotional strength to withstand the pressures of a three- to four-hour game. It demands compatibility among players as well as trust and confidence in others' directions and decisions. Finally, it requires total involvement.

It provides comradeship, friendship and a better understanding and acceptance of others. It can teach players to lose well and win well, and to be genuine in their congratulations, regardless of whether a winner or a loser. It can offer contact over a wide age range and promote a greater acceptance of individuals of different age groups. It can offer gentle relaxation or the excitement of intense rivalry.

Of course, other sports could lay claim to such advantages, but bowls has its own particular rewards, from the enjoyment of playing as an individual to the team involvement of the rink. It is recognized as one of the fastest-growing games in Britain, and perhaps that fact is the best advertisement for what the game has to offer.

Appendix

THE ENGLISH BOWLS COACHING SCHEME

The EBCS was formed in 1979, and its aim was, and is still, to improve standards of performance in English bowls by the use of certificated instructors and coaches. All instructors and coaches first have to attend a structured course and are finally assessed as to their ability to coach bowlers over a wide range of ability and performance.

Instructors are, in the main, prepared for the important task of introducing complete beginners to the game of bowls. Coaches are faced with other tasks such as developing tactics and strategies and running coaching clinics, where individual bowlers can seek assistance when they know that their performance in the game has deteriorated for one reason or another. Coaches are also prepared to offer purposeful practices, personal practices, and positional practices for groups or individual bowlers.

The acceptance of coaching in the game of bowls has now reached a level where certain clubs will only entertain application for membership from a beginner after the new bowler has completed the introductory sessions given by the club instructor. It is now increasingly common for clubs to invite groups of coaches to provide their members with coaching sessions aimed at improving standards generally. Some counties have invited coaches to produce programmes of coaching activities to help prepare county teams before important matches. This is also the case with international squads, where the National Coaching Team assist them in their preparation for an international series.

The concept of coaching in the game of bowls is still very young by comparison with other sports, which makes the acceptance of it by bowlers and clubs all the more gratifying.

None of this would have been achieved without a great deal of hard work and dedication by those instructors and coaches prepared by the EBCS. In 1979, the EBCS was structured along the lines of having a national director, supported by six regional coaches working closely with each of their county coaches. Since I receive many requests for information from people who either wish to take up the game or to become qualified under the scheme, or even those who want some information about coaching generally, I thought it would be useful to include the following names and addresses.

Appendix

Regional and County Coaches

Southern Region

Regional Coach
Peter A. Line
Flat 2, Elm Court
53 Westwood Road
Southampton
Hampshire SO2 1DX

Middlesex County Coaches
F. Jeffreys
62b Audley Road
Hendon
Middlesex NW4 3HB

Mrs B. Jones
35 The Chase
Eastcote
Pinner
Middlesex HA5 1SJ

Sussex County Coaches
W.F. Nippers
5 Harmers Hay Road
Hailsham
Sussex BN27 1TM

Mrs S. Flegg
50 St. Peters Road
Littlehampton
Sussex BN17 6BB

Surrey County Coaches
L. Stevens
30 Tudor Close
Cheam
Surrey SM3 8QT

Mrs P. Ward
7 Cedars Road
Beddington
Surrey CR0 4FU

Kent County Coaches
N.D. Evenden
6 Forge Lane
Horton Kirby
Nr. Dartford
Kent DA4 9DF

Mrs D. Kennedy
2 Hunters Chase
Whitstable
Kent CT5 4QD

Wiltshire County Coach
H. Clark
65 Heathfield
Chippenham
Wiltshire SN15 1BH

Isle of Wight County Coach
Mrs I. Pearse
'Burwood'
Harts Hill
Wellow
IOW 5

Hampshire County Coaches
E. Jones
35 Beechwood Crescent
Chandlers Ford
Eastleigh
Hampshire SO5 1PF

Mrs P. Powell
'Archways'
Alexandria Road
Sutton Scotney
Winchester
Hampshire SO21 3LF

Midlands Region

Regional Coach

V.F. Cooper
534 Kettering Road North
Northampton
Northamptonshire NN3 1HN

Derbyshire County Coach

S. Whittaker
24 Cromwell Road
Derby
Derbyshire DE3 6TR

Leicester County Coaches

J.R. Yates
25 Herbert Avenue
Leicester
Leicestershire LE4 4PE

Mrs M. Hendry
8 Watergate Lane
Braunstone
Leicestershire LE3 2XP

Lincolnshire

G. Mazingham
10 Keadby Close
Hartsholme Estate
Lincoln LN6 0DZ

Northamptonshire County Coaches

P. Harris
70 Banbury Road
Brackley
Northamptonshire NN13 6AT

Mrs C. Barlow
123 Billing Road
Northampton
Northamptonshire NN1 5RR

Nottinghamshire County Coaches

J. Berrington
33 Overdale Road
Stockhill Estate
Nottinghamshire

K. Euerby
550 Woodborough Road
Mapperley
Nottinghamshire NG3 5FH

Warwickshire County Coach

D. Lanchbury
17 Grange Gardens
Wellesbourne
Nr. Warwickshire
CV3 9RL

South West Region

Regional Coach

Gwyn John
'Gower'
34 Ocean View Road
Bude
Cornwall EX23 8NN

Dorset County Coach

J. Chislett
4 Kenmoor Close
Weymouth
Dorset DT3 6JZ

Devon County Coach

L. Fisher
1A Kingshurst Drive
Paignton
Devon

Appendix

Cornwall County Coach
D. James
29 Wheal Gorland Road
St. Day
Redruth
Cornwall TR16 5LT

Somerset County Coach
E. Ward
16 Clevedon Road
Portishead
Bristol
Avon BS20 8PH

Northern Region

Regional Coach
Derek Bell
101 Station Lane
Seaton Carew
Hartlepool
Cleveland TS25 1EX

Lancashire County Coach
A. Drury
75 Belvedere Road
Thornton Cleveleys
Blackpool
Lancashire SY5 5DF

Yorkshire County Coach
G. Dash
10 Ashby Close
Westborough Way
Hull
Yorkshire HU4 7SP

Cumbria County Coach
F. Allason
'Edenvale'
Tree Terrace
Brampton
Cumbria CA8 1TY

Northumberland County Coach
J. Ferguson
3 Dene Crescent
South Gosforth
Newcastle upon Tyne
Northumberland NE3 1QS

East Anglia

Regional Coach
Arthur Meeson
22 Pleasant Rise
Hatfield
Hertfordshire AL9 5DU

Bedfordshire County Coach
W. Corless
28 Braithwaite Court
Malzeard Road
Luton
Bedfordshire LU3 1BE

Cambridgeshire County Coach
V. Purse
18 High Street
Coton
Cambridgeshire CB3 7PL

Essex County Coach
R. Casey
25 Benfleet Park Road
South Benfleet
Essex SS7 5HG

Hertfordshire County Coach
A. Meeson
22 Pleasant Rise
Hatfield
Hertfordshire AL9 5DU

Huntingdon County Coach
K.S. Parker
3 Laughtons Lane
Houghton
Huntingdon
Cambridgeshire PE17 2AT

Norfolk County Coach
B. Warnes
188 Middleton Road
Gorleston-on-Sea
Norfolk NR31 7PX

Suffolk County Coach
P. Jones
21 Wren Close
Mildenhall
Bury St. Edmunds
Suffolk IP28 7HH

Central Region

Regional Coach
A. Hodgkinson
4 Pensfield Park
Charlton Mead Estate
Bristol
Avon BS10 6LD

Berkshire County Coach
E. Brown
169 Rodway Road
Reading
Berkshire RG3 6EN

Buckinghamshire County Coach
D.F. Laing
54 Copthall Lane
Chalfont-St-Peter
Buckinghamshire SO9 0DJ

Gloucestershire County Coach
A. Hodgkinson
4 Pensfield Park
Charlton Mead Est.
Bristol
Avon BS10 6LD

Herefordshire County Coach
I. Maddox
20 Newton Close
Deer Park
Ledbury
Hereford and Worcester HR8 2XG

Oxfordshire County Council
G. Rowell
38 Waverley Avenue
Kidlington
Oxford
Oxfordshire OX5 2NA

Worcestershire County Coach
K. Stanton
68 Wellington Road
Bromsgrove
Worcestershire B60 2AX

Note The Address for the National Director of the EBCS, who is the author of this book, is included under Useful Addresses on page 118.

The above represent only a fraction of the four thousand instructors and seven hundred and sixty coaches who have qualified under the scheme, but they are the group who have to administer, organize and generally oversee the coaching activities undertaken in their counties or regions. Such responsibilities are onerous enough but then there is also to be taken into consideration the coaching they do themselves. The EBCS depends greatly on each instructor and coach fulfilling all the demands that are made upon them. They have to be prepared to give of that most precious commodity – time. The coaching skills they have to offer are freely given, and their real reward is to be able to help bowlers overcome or solve problems. However, be assured that no coach can help any player to improve unless that player is motivated enough to want to improve. If you feel that your game can benefit in some way from working with a coach, then you must approach that coach with total honesty. Unless this is done, it will be virtually impossible for the coach to be of any real assistance.

The EBCS embraces all codes of bowls, including crown green bowls. All who qualify under the scheme are looked upon as bowls coaches, and not segregated according to the particular code they play. There are an ever-increasing number of women qualifying under the coaching scheme and offering their skills at instructor or coach level, and this is a very welcome development.

Coaching seminars at regional and county level are held throughout the year. The majority of the National Coaching Squad travel all over the country to inform coaches and instructors of the most up-to-date developments in bowls coaching. Attendance at such Seminars can vary in number from forty to one hundred or more. In this way, information of all kinds is passed on to those people upon whom the EBCS depends so much. In the main, such seminars are of a very practical nature with the bulk of the programme taking place on the green.

The EBCS exists to provide a service for all bowlers of all codes. As a body, it is proud of its achievements and the reputation it has among bowlers. Already there are many hundreds of players who can testify that they have been assisted in some way or other through the help of a coach, and that their enjoyment of the game has been enhanced. It is hoped that many more will seek to benefit from the skills of instructors and coaches, so that standards in all areas of the game can be further improved.

Any success that the EBCS has achieved must be attributed in the main to two people: Mr H.A.C. Death, the Chairman of the Scheme, and Jimmy Davidson, its first National Director of Coaching. Their vision, determination and dedication were responsible for the introduction of the Coaching Scheme, its aims, its structure and its eventual acceptance.

Glossary

Back Bowl A bowl that has come to rest beyond the jack or the main body of bowls in the head.

Backhand When, for the right-handed player, the bowl is delivered so that the curve of the bowl is from left to right as it moves towards its objective.

Bank The outer wall of the ditch that surrounds the green. It is raised above the playing surface.

Be up The same as 'Do not be short', only more emphatic.

Bias That which is inbuilt into the bowl and causes the bowl to travel in a curve.

Block or stopper A bowl delivered with the correct pace to stop short of the objective, in the hope that it will prevent an opponent being able to play a certain shot.

Bowls Usually a set of four identical bowls, manufactured under strictly controlled specifications. It is essential that bowlers choose a set which they can use with the greatest ease and comfort.

Centre line An imaginary line that runs lengthwise down the centre of the rink.

Counter Any bowl which contributes to the score at the completion of the end.

Cover that bowl An instruction to a bowler to bowl in such a way that the bowl finishes between the jack and the bowl indicated.

Dead bowl Either a bowl which comes to rest in the ditch or is knocked into the ditch and is not a toucher, or a bowl that comes to rest outside the confines of the rink, either in its course or by being knocked there.

Dead end An end which is considered not to have been played and so no score is recorded. It can happen as a result of the jack being driven out of the confines of the playing area.

Delivery The moment at which the bowl leaves the hand.

Ditch The depression that surrounds the green. Its edge marks the boundary of the playing surface. Measurements of the ditch need to conform to the laws of the game.

Do not be short A plea to a bowler to use sufficient pace to reach his objective.

Draw The path the bowl will travel to reach its objective.

Draw the shot To deliver a bowl at the correct pace or weight, and with the correct green or land, to arrive exactly at its objective.

End The sequence of play, beginning with the placing of the mat and ending with the coming to rest of the last player's bowl,

Glossary

after all have delivered their bowls in the same direction.

Fast green   Usually a dry and closely cut surface which offers little resistance to the progress of the bowl.

Fire or drive   A shot where the bowl is delivered at a very fast pace.

Fluke   A shot excruciatingly executed, yet sublimely successful – do at least say sorry!

Follow through   This should be the natural movement forward of the delivery arm following the line or path of the bowl.

Foot fault   When the rear foot is not completely on or above the mat at the moment of delivery. The player could incur a penalty.

Forehand   When, for the right-handed player, the bowl is delivered so that the curve of the bowl is from right to left as it travels towards its objective.

Green   The total playing surface, the measurements of which are laid down in the rules.

Green line   The curved line that the bowl must travel from the mat to reach its objective.

Head   The jack and as many bowls as have been played at any stage of any end. Bowls in the head may be on the rink or in the ditch.

Heavy bowl   Where a bowl has been delivered with too much pace and will end beyond its objective.

Jack or kitty   The round white ball towards which play is directed. The size of the jack must conform to the rules.

Jack-High bowl   A bowl which, when it comes to rest, is at the same distance from the mat as is the jack.

Lead   The player who lays the mat, rolls the jack, and delivers the first bowl in an end. He may sometimes toss the coin at the beginning of the game to determine which team has the right to start play.

Live bowl   Any bowl that comes to rest within the confines of the rink and is acceptable under the conditions laid down by the laws of the game, or any toucher in the ditch.

Long jack   A jack that is the greatest distance allowed from the front edge of the mat, or is close to this limit.

Mark it or chalk it   To mark a toucher with chalk.

Marker   A person who undertakes to see that a game of singles is played according to the rules. He marks all touchers, centres the jack, measures, and keeps the score. During the playing of an end, it could be wiser for the marker not to talk to the players unless asked a direct question.

Mat   The mat from which a bowler must make his delivery (the size is laid down in the rules).

Measure   A device used to determine which bowl is nearest the jack.

Measuring   The process of determining which bowl is nearest the jack.

Narrow shot Where a player has not allowed enough green or land. But this shot can sometimes be played intentionally.

Open it up An instruction for a bowl to be delivered with enough pace to clear any obstruction in the way of bowls that are between the player and the jack.

Pace or weight The amount of force with which the bowl is delivered to execute a particular shot.

Pace of the green *See* fast green and slow green.

Pairs Two players against two, each using four bowls for a period of twenty-one ends. Their positions in order of play: lead and then skip.

Penalty This may be awarded by the umpire when, for example, a player has foot faulted in delivering his bowl. The umpire could also declare the bowl to be dead.

Plant shot When a player bowls his bowl to strike other bowls which could be in line, in order to gain his objective.

Promote this bowl An instruction to a bowler to play his bowl onto a bowl belonging to his side, so that the bowl that was stationary is pushed closer to the objective.

Push and rest The bowling of a bowl with sufficient pace or weight that it pushes a bowl from its position, so that the position is taken by the last bowl delivered.

Rest this bowl An instruction to a player to bring his bowl to rest against another bowl.

Rink The rectangular area of the green on which play takes place.

Rink of players or fours A group of four players against four, each bowling two bowls for a period of twenty-one ends. Their positions in order of play: lead, second, third and skip.

Rub off A bowl that, during its running course, comes into light contact with another, which can affect the line of direction.

Scorer The person, in a match between teams or sides, who is responsible for keeping the current scores on the master score-board.

Second or number two The player who plays after the lead in a game of fours or triples. He marks the score-card and keeps the score-board up to date.

Second bowl The bowl which finishes closest to the jack, other than the shot bowl.

Short bowl A bowl that has not been delivered with sufficient pace to reach its objective.

Short jack A jack that is at the shortest distance allowed from the front edge of the mat, or close to this limit.

Shot The bowl that finishes nearest to the jack at any stage of play.

Shoulder of the green That point on the green where the bowl begins to curve inwards towards its objective.

Side or team An agreed number of players whose combined scores determine the result of a match.

Glossary

Singles One player against one player, each using four bowls.

Skip The captain of a game of fours, triples or pairs. He is last to bowl and is responsible for dictating the tactics of the game.

Slow or heavy green Where the surface offers some greater resistance to the progress of the bowl.

Split these bowls An instruction to the bowler to bowl a bowl of sufficient pace that it forces apart other bowls, and has enough momentum to carry on beyond that point.

Stance The position adopted by the bowler on the mat, prior to delivery.

String Normally a green 'string' drawn tightly along the green to define the boundaries of the rink.

Take it out An instruction to a bowler to bowl with sufficient pace to push an opponent's bowl away.

Taking green or land On forehand or backhand, the bowler bowls to the shoulder so that his bowl will curve and come to rest as near as possible to the point he desires.

Third A position in a game of fours. He will deputize for his skip in certain circumstances, and could be responsible for measuring.

Tied end When the nearest bowls of both sides are exactly the same distance from the jack at the completion of the end (e.g. when both have a bowl actually touching the jack). Neither side scores but it is a

completed end and is entered on the score-card.

Toucher in the ditch A toucher (see below) which has fallen into the ditch. This is a 'live' bowl, unless it has come to rest outside the confines of the rink.

Toucher on the green A bowl which, during its course, has touched the jack, or a bowl which has come to rest and falls over to touch the jack before the next bowl is delivered, or a bowl that is the last to be delivered and falls and touches the jack within the period of half a minute. All the above will be marked with a chalk mark.

Trail the jack To play a bowl in order to move the jack to another position on the rink.

Triples Three players against three, each using three bowls for a playing period of eighteen ends. Their positions in order of play: lead, second and skip.

Umpire The person with total overall authority during a game to enforce the laws of the game.

Using the mat The movement of the mat (within the limits of the rules) for the purposes of lengthening or shortening the length of the jack.

Wick off A bowl that is travelling at a certain pace which comes into an angled contact with another bowl, thus causing the course of the moving bowl to be definitely altered.

Wide bowl Where the player has allowed too much green or land for his bowl.

Wouldn't crack an egg A bowl delivered with insufficient pace to achieve its end.

Wrecked An attempted shot, frustrated by contact with another bowl which lay between the mat and the jack.

Wrest this bowl out An instruction to bowl a bowl with sufficient pace to push another bowl sufficiently from its former position.

Useful Addresses

English Bowling Association
Mr D. Johnson
The Secretary
Lyndhurst Road
Worthing
West Sussex
BN11 2AZ

English Women's Bowling Association
Mrs N. Colling
The Secretary
'Daracombe'
The Clays
Market Lavington
Wiltshire
SN10 4AY

English Indoor Bowling Association
Mr B. Telfer
The Secretary
290A Barking Road
London
E6 3BA

English Women's Indoor Bowling Association
Mrs P. Allison
The Secretary
8 Oakfield Road
Carterton
Oxford
OX8 3RB

English Bowls Federation
Mr J. Webb
The Secretary
62 Frampton Place
Boston
Lincolnshire
PE21 8EL

English Women's Bowls Federation
Mrs I. Younger
The Secretary
'Irela'
Holborn Crescent
Ryton
Tyne and Wear
NE40 3DH

English Bowls Coaching Scheme
Mr Gwyn John
The National Director
'Gower'
34 Ocean View Road
Bude
Cornwall
EX23 8NN

Index

Index

The Skills of the Game Series

American Football	Les Wilson
Badminton	Peter Roper
Basketball	Paul Stimpson
Canoeing	Neil Shave
Cricket	Keith Andrew
Cross-Country Skiing	Paddy Field & Tim Walker
Crown Green Bowls	Harry Barratt
Endurance Running	Norman Brook
Fitness for Sport	Rex Hazeldine
Golf	John Stirling
Gymnastics	Trevor Low
Hockey	John Cadman
Judo	Tony Reay
Jumping	Malcolm Arnold
Karate	Vic Charles
Netball	Betty Galsworthy
Orienteering	Carol McNeill
Rhythmic Gymnastics	Jenny Bott
Rowing	Rosie Mayglothling
Rugby League	Maurice Bamford
Rugby Union	Barrie Corless
Skiing	John Shedden
Soccer	Tony Book
Sprinting and Hurdling	Peter Warden
Squash	Ian McKenzie
Strength Training for Sport	Rex Hazeldine
Swimming	John Verrier
Table Tennis	Gordon Steggall
Tennis	Charles Applewhaite & Bill Moss
Throwing	Max Jones
Trampolining	Brian & Erika Phelps
Triathlon	Steve Trew
Volleyball	Keith Nicholls
Water Skiing	John West
Windsurfing	Ben Oakley
Women's Lacrosse	Bobbie Trafford & Kath Howarth

Further details of titles available or in preparation can be obtained from the publishers.